Herring Girls and Hiring Fairs

Memories of the Northumberland coast and countryside

Maureen Brook

Tyne Bridge Publishing

Acknowledgements

The author would like to thank the following: the many people who shared their memories of past times and made me so welcome. Barbara Wright, Bill Telfer and Margaret Aitken who kindly offered family photos. Dennis Orton of Westwood, Bardon Mill, for sharing his wealth of knowledge concerning farming methods. Ruth Forster of Stocksfield, for allowing me free access to her many family papers and the records concerning rural crafts. The Bardon Mill WEA Group whose enthusiasm for the material prompted me into writing it up for a wider audience. The members of the Hadston History Group who gave me much information on day-to-day life in a rural mining community. I would also like to thank my husband, Fred, for his endless patience which was matched only by that of Anna Flowers and Vanessa Histon at Tyne Bridge Publishing.

Illustrations are reproduced from the collections of Newcastle Libraries unless otherwise indicated.

Map of Northumberland by Katherine Pentney

© Maureen Brook, 2005

Published by
City of Newcastle upon Tyne
Newcastle Libraries, Information & Lifelong Learning Service
Tyne Bridge Publishing
2005

ISBN: 1 85795 147 6
        (978 1 85795 147 6)

www.tynebridgepublishing.co.uk

Printed by Elanders Hindson, North Tyneside

Front cover: Haymakers, Coxlodge, 1902.
Back cover: Alnmouth fishermen c.1910.
Opposite page: Beadnell c.1930.

The recipes on pages 15 and 17 are adapted from *With a Northumbrian Flavour: A Northern Cookbook* by Barbara Stephenson (Newcastle Libraries, 1992).

Sheepshearing at Beadnell, c.1902.

Contents

Berwick upon Tweed

Holy Island

A697

A1

Coldstream

Kelso

The county of Northumberland and some of the places mentioned in this book.

Bamburgh

North Sunderland & Seahouses

Beadnell

A68

Yetholm

Wooler

Newton by the Sea

Jedburgh

Chathill

Longhoughton

The North Sea

Kidlandlee

Alnwick

Lesbury

Alnmouth

Linn Briggs

Alwinton

Northumberland

Harbottle

Rothbury

Amble

Longframlington

Broomhill/Hadston/ Red Row/ East Chevington

East Wilkwood

Kielder Water

Otterburn

Coldrife

Ashington

Elsdon

North Tyne

Netherwitton

Newbiggin

Bellingham

A696

Morpeth

Blagdon

A68

Blyth

A1

Seaton Delaval

Roman Wall

Whitley Bay

North Shields

Haydon Bridge

Tynemouth

South Shields

Haltwhistle

Corbridge

Newcastle

Henshaw/ Bardon Mill/ Tow House

Hexham

A69

Gateshead

River Tyne

South Tyne

Allendale

Sunderland

Whittonstall

'In those days …'

A few years ago, I paid a visit to Cragside, Rothbury (former home of Lord Armstrong and now a National Trust property) with my mother. The Victorian kitchens were full of visitors from all over the world, many of them staring at the various gadgets on display and wondering aloud about their functions. Irritated by this ignorance, Mollie, my late mother (embarrassing me just as she had done when I was young) stepped into the roped-off section of the kitchen and proceeded to give a lecture on these utensils. Her audience was enchanted and for Mollie (born in 1914, the daughter of a Newcastle tram driver) it was a chance to show off everything she had learned as a housekeeper during the 1930s.

It struck me later that all around me in my home county was a wealth of knowledge of past times which would very soon be lost. And so, the idea for this book was sparked off. Letters went out to care homes all over the county asking for elderly people willing to share their memories; organisations such as the Women's Institute and Rotary Clubs were approached and, as word went round, personal introductions were offered and letters arrived with names of more volunteers. Carrying my trusty tape-recorder with me, off I went to meet the lively people who contributed details of their lives. I found that this is a county in which many people stay put. They may move around the area generally but do not like to be too far away from their own locality. I met a Pegswood man who had not been outside his village for twenty years and, I suspect, there are many others like him. Conversely, when people did decide to leave the county, they took their skills all over the world; I was surprised to learn of several whose male relatives had taken their mining expertise to Mexico. A sizeable proportion of my contributors had relatives in far-flung places, but Northumberland itself remains a far-flung, relatively empty county. Unlike more populous places in Britain, it is not hard

The market town of Hexham nestles in the Tyne Valley (from an old postcard).

to find someone, provided you know who to ask.

The memories you will find in this book come mostly from the early years of the 20th century. They speak of times and customs which suggest a more serene age than the one in which we now live, though many lives were very hard, and some some of my contributors had difficult, even tragic circumstances to contend with. They are extremely personal recollections and, as such, sometimes evoke rose-tinted days of youth and vigour; keep in mind, however, that the outside world throughout this period was a turbulent place, it simply intruded less forcefully than it does now in this age of the mass media. There was also a considerable gulf between the lives of the rich and the poor in the early part of the century and it is

A Northumberland farm around 1930. This little boy would live through a world of change.

surprising that these differences seem not to have brought about great envy amongst the contributors. Their lives were so separate, so very different, that the they seemed unable to appreciate the economic gap in any but the most superficial terms – for them it was just how things were.

With luck, we too will be telling our grandchildren, and possibly great-grandchildren, of the peculiarities of our own surroundings. What was commonplace to us may strike them as extremely strange. As children, my contributors could hardly imagine a time when horses would not be an everyday sight, sound and smell on the roads. People rode on bicycles, in carts, carriages and traps – all familiar sights. The

prospect of the new-fangled telephones being available to everyone was inconceivable, as it was for many people during the first half of the 20th century. Now they are carried by everyone. Thinking machines (computers) belonged strictly to science fiction in a time when the typewriter and sewing machine were relatively new inventions. And what of the credit card – paying, not with good old pounds, shillings and pence, but with a plastic card for goods marked in an entirely different currency which has 100 pence to the pound, rather than 240 pennies? It was a different world.

Maureen Brook, 2005

Family ties

'Lots of girls played with the end of a long skipping rope in one hand, whilst they balanced a bairn on the hip with the other.'

A few of the people featured in this book were brought up in affluent surroundings where maids, kitchen staff, laundry women or daily helps were an accepted part of life. The great majority, however, lived in conditions which today would be regarded as intolerable. Cottages were overcrowded and lacking in the most basic of amenities; parents laboured endlessly to keep large families decently clothed and tolerably fed. For example, Mrs Isabella Keen (born in Alnwick in 1902 and the daughter of a hind – a Northumbrian annually-contracted farmworker) had four brothers and six sisters. The girls slept three to a bed, in two beds with straw-filled mattresses, which were crammed into an upstairs room. The boys slept two to a bed in the other bedroom. Mrs Keen's parents had a 'press' bed – a large, pull-out drawer in the kitchen press – in the single downstairs room. At the bottom of the garden was an ash midden; outside the house was a cold tap.

With hindsight, the people in this book now appreciate the struggle their parents had to raise them and marvel at the closeness and harmony they managed to create in such circumstances. With only a few exceptions they describe the home atmosphere as loving and warm.

Robbie McKenna (born at Coldrife in 1902, the son of a stonemason) recounts: 'There were ten of us. My father would come home after a long, hard day's work in the quarry and then start on the garden, poor soul. It was a big garden; he grew all the vegetables and fruit we ate. And mother, she never stopped. Even when she sat down at night and took her apron off, she'd be darning or mending, knitting, or making clippy mats for the floor.'

Gardening was an essential source of food for the family. This photograph, probably showing an allotment, dates from c.1930.

'They weren't at all demonstrative: they'd have been horrified if you kissed or cuddled them, or anything like that. We were taught, from being little, to keep our feelings to ourselves. In fact, when I was a little lad, I was terrified that my mother would die afore me and I'd shame the family by crying at her funeral. No, there was no hugging, but we knew they were warm and loving. They made us feel content.

'Mother and Father were strict with us; they taught us right from wrong and you didn't want to displease them by being naughty. We weren't smacked at all; a dark frown was enough to make us feel miserable. But we were loved. I suppose that it was really that you felt accepted just as you were. Probably in a big family – and there were ten of us – there wasn't the time to want any of us to be something we weren't.'

Whilst Robbie dreaded 'dark frowns', May Telfer (a farmer's daughter from North Sunderland, born in 1903 remembers, 'When Daddy called me "my lady", I knew I was in trouble. There would be harsh words, but my real punishment was in feeling wretched for upsetting my parents.'

After obedience, contentment was a much-prized virtue; envy a despicable vice. Mrs Cassie (born in Longhoughton in 1904, a hind's child) remembered her sister being given a china doll. Mrs Cassie coveted the doll to the point of misery. The old lady next door, feeling some sympathy, brought her a wooden doll as a substitute, but Mrs Cassie chopped it up and was given a sound smacking for doing so.

A family of eight children around 1920.

'All the same, on Christmas morning, there was a cloth doll (made from a sock) in my stocking. Mother had made it for me, because she knew that I was so jealous of Bertha's doll that it was souring me.'

It was common to have seven or eight surviving children, or even more. Mrs Turnbull, born at Melkridge in 1916, whose father was a master shaft sinker for the local collieries, was the youngest of ten – and claims to have been spoiled by her older siblings. Sally (born in Chathill, 1902), was a shepherd's daughter, fourth in a family of 14 and the eldest girl. She remembers helping her mother to cook, wash, sew and mend from an early age. She was also trusted to attend to the latest baby, or to take the toddlers out to play: 'Lots of girls played with the end of a long skipping rope in one hand, whilst they balanced a bairn on the hip with the other.'

Parents themselves were often members of large families, so only children were seldom lonely, surrounded as they were by cousins, nephews and nieces of a similar age with whom they could play. Where there was single child, it was frequently because other babies failed to survive or, most tragically, because the mother died in childbirth.

Mrs Buglass (born at Berwick in 1902, a farmer and butcher's daughter) was the only surviving child of three born to her parents. Her mother died giving birth to the stillborn third baby. Mrs Buglass was not quite a year old at the time.

The Ditchburns of Ashington were about to improve

their prospects by moving south. Jimmy Ditchburn's (born 1924) father was a gardener who had just obtained a new position 'at one of them big houses – Woburn, I think.' The family's possessions were all packed and ready when Jimmy's father was stricken by appendicitis on the day before the move. He died of peritonitis, leaving his widow with two boys under three.

Ada Foggin's (born at Seaton Delaval, 1908) father was a miner, with great ambitions for himself. Encouraged by his own mother, who lent him the money for his passage, he emigrated to Australia and was never heard from again. He left behind him a wife, two small daughters and a mountain of debt to be paid off.

Often when a parent was widowed or abandoned, the child (or children) was cared for by grandparents or other relatives. Mrs Buglass was brought up by her paternal grandparents – her grandfather was Berwick's Sanitary Officer – until her father remarried when she was ten years old.

Jimmy Ditchburn's mother moved into a smaller flat in the same Ashington street as her parents and a married sister, all of whom helped out by feeding and looking after her sons while she worked.

Mrs Foggin and her sister were handed over to a grandmother and unmarried sister who lived inland in Morpeth. Their mother went back into live-in service and her wages paid for their keep. She saw her

girls only once a month from then on.

Children were rarely abandoned. On the whole, families regarded it as their Christian Duty to look after their own. Duty was an important ethical concept – not just one's duty to King or Queen and Country, but duty to parents, family, employers and, in some cases, employees.

Mrs Mildred Wright (born 1912), the daughter of bank manager in Wooler, recalled a sharp lesson on duty and respect delivered by her father.

'I'd be about ten or so. Every week we had an old lady

Mrs J. Briggs

The kitchen, with its range, was the heart of family life; photographed by Edwin Flowers-Luck.

come in to polish the silver. I made the mistake of calling her by her Christian name, which was what all the adults did, but my father was very cross with me. He slapped me sharply and said, "If Miss Pattison does us the honour of coming in to clean our silver, she deserves our respect, young lady!" At the time I cried, but I never forgot the lesson.'

Most of all though, there was one's duty to God. Christian churches, of whatever denomination, played a pivotal part in the lives of families and many of the earliest memories of the children are connected to the church.

'My first memory is of standing on the seat in church and Daddy was very cross with me. I'd be about three. Grandfather was an Elder of the Presbyterian church and it wasn't done for me to misbehave like that. We learned to sit still and not to fidget at an early age.' (May Telfer)

'Grandmother's housekeeper would dress me in a freshly-starched white pinafore with frilly shoulders, then stand back and make sure I was presentable, before handing me over to Grandpa to go to church.' (Mrs Buglass of Berwick was the darling of her paternal grandparents who cared for her for ten years.)

Margaret Douglas (born at Amble in 1902, a miner's daughter) recalls how solemn Sundays were, 'My father was a Methodist lay-preacher. Much of our lives revolved around Chapel. He was the leader of the Band of Hope and my twin sister and I signed The Pledge (a solemn vow of temperance) before we were six years old.

'Mother was a staunch "British Woman" – they were pledged to uphold the highest family standards and to abjure strong drink. She would cook on Sundays, but would not thread a needle because that was her work during the week, her being a dressmaker. No, if a button flew off father's jack-et on Sunday morning before he was due to preach, then it stayed off, that was it!'

For Bob Duff, born at North Shields in 1910, the son of a trawlerman, it was, 'Christ Church every Sunday morning, Sunday School in the afternoon, then Evening Service. Choir Practice twice a week – me and me brothers were all in the church choir.'

Bob's experience is similar to that of May Douglas, born in 1920, in Bamburgh, at the northern end of the county, 'Church three times on Sunday with Grandma. The old ladies all wore long, black skirts.'

Rob McKenna's (born 1902, a stonemason's son) family at Coldrife were Roman Catholics and lived at some distance from the nearest church; their formal worship was more sporadic. 'At Whitehouse, they'd turn the barn into a church. Paddy Timmins would ring a bell and we'd go over there once a month. The priest walked over from Thropton and he'd come to our house for a dram on the way back.'

The third Commandment is 'Honour thy father and thy mother' so family duty also included looking after aged parents. Life expectancy was lower: few grandparents survived until their grandchildren were adults. No-one remembered a great-grandparent. Mrs Buglass, in the care of her grandparents after her mother's death, lost her grandmother when she was six years old, and then her grandfather when she was ten. The demise of both parents must have put considerable pressure on her father to find someone to care for his daughter: he remarried later in that year.

Aged parents dreaded being a financial burden on their children, but they also dreaded the workhouse which separated long-married couples. However thrifty a couple might be, low wages meant that it was not always possible to save for old age. For those whose work was low paid or seasonal – for example, stonemasons (like Robbie McKenna's father) who could be laid off for weeks in winter – saving for retirement was a real problem. Many elderly people continued working until well into their seventies.

Old Age Pensions were not introduced until 1908: At first, they were non-contributory and provided five shillings a week for those over 70, whose income was under 10 shillings a week. There was a sliding scale, the pension falling by a shilling per week for those whose income reached 12 shillings a week. To put this into perspective: agricultural wages averaged around two shillings and sixpence a week in 1908. Farm workers had some perks which I'll discuss later in Chapter 8, but for the 'labouring classes', as they were known, it was a cash-starved life. Some old people stubbornly refused to accept the State Pension; for them it smacked too much of the Poor Law of their youth. In these cases, adult offspring were essential for support. Robbie McKenna remembers an elderly couple living in a tar shack not too far from where they lived: a very rural setting, within sight of the southern end of the Simonside Hills: 'My mother did her best to help them, but she had her own family and

Wooler around 1920. The local parish church was central to most people's lives.

they refused to take the food from our mouths. Instead, they starved themselves to death.'

For an old person without family, pre-1908, once savings were exhausted, it was either the Workhouse or starvation. As Robbie McKenna says, some chose the latter.

What is also remarkable is that, given the size and proximity of families, few major rifts occurred between them. When they did, they were sometimes long-lasting and could have serious consequences in a social framework which relied so heavily on the extended family. Parents often insisted on continued obedience to their wishes from adult children – particularly from their daughters. Defiance could lead to rejection, as it did in the case of Mrs T's mother.

Born in Wooler in 1904, third in a family of five, Mrs T's father, a miner, was killed in a Bedlington pit accident when she was very young. Her maternal grandmother lived next door to the family and took over the raising of the children whilst their mother went out to work. When Mrs T was eight years old, her mother decided to remarry, but grandmother thoroughly disapproved of her daughter's choice of second husband and threatened to wash her hands of the whole family if the marriage went ahead.

As it happened, Grandmother's judgement proved sound, although her subsequent actions were considerably less wise. Mrs T's mother died in childbirth, leaving the children of her first marriage in the care of a drunkard stepfather. Grandmother loathed the man and continued to have nothing to do with him or the family.

The elder girl left school and home as soon as she was allowed to and took a live-in job in another part of the country. Mrs T's older brother, meanwhile, was bullied into working on a farm after his shift at the pit. Finally, he too left home.

There followed a succession of 'aunts' – women who were brought home for the night. Grandmother still refused to 'interfere'. The step-father then moved a 'housekeeper' and her ten-year-old son into the house. Mrs T and her small brother and sister found themselves on starvation rations while the 'housekeeper's' child grew fat. The relationship between the step-father and his mistress ended in an acrimo-nious row over her theft of his money. The two remaining girls and their brother rejoiced greatly at her departure.

At that point, at not quite twelve years old, Mrs T's life became utterly unbearable. Sexual abuse was not a subject any decent person would discuss and the only way Mrs T could escape was to beg her teacher to issue her with a labour certificate so that she could leave school, even though she was under-age. She pleaded that the family needed her money since her stepfather had been sacked for drunkenness. Aged just twelve, she left school and home and found work as a live-in domestic on a farm. The younger brother fol-lowed suit and when her eldest sister wrote to say that she was married, Mrs T arranged for her to adopt the ten year-old sister who remained at home.

Mrs T had to grow up very quickly. She has always despised the drunken stepfather who abused her and still bit-terly resents her grandmother for turning a blind eye to the children's plight, just to prove that she had been right.

Agricultural Employment.

SITUATIONS VACANT.

REPECTABLE Girl Wanted for Farm House, near Morpeth; references required.—Write Box 61, Journal Office. 7564

SINGLE Man Wanted as Shepherd-Stockman.—Write Box A.32, Journal Office. 7591

STRONG Lad, 16-18 years, Wanted; able to milk preferred.—Jordan, High Highlaws, Morpeth. 7636

STRONG Girl Wanted; able to milk, and assist in delivery of milk.—Amos, South Farm, Wardley, Pelaw. L.595

Work to be had for farm girls: Newcastle Journal, May 1929.

Housekeeping

'Yorkshire puddings as light as angels' wings.'

For most of the contributors, home was the place where mother worked endlessly at cleaning, mending, darning, knitting, baking and cooking. The week had a regular pattern: Monday was washday. After a dripping sandwich for breakfast (dripping was the remains of the fat and juices from the Sunday joint; the brown juices which settled at the bottom of the dripping jar were particularly prized), schoolchildren would set off for school to the sound of the pounding of poss-sticks in poss tubs (pictured on page 15) and the smell of hot, soapy water in the air. An anxious eye was also kept on the weather, for rain could mean the house would be filled with damp sheets and clothing for the rest of the week.

The woman of the house rose at 6 a.m. in order to fill the set pot (a copper boiler). Sheets would already be soaking in the stone sink.

For town wives, filling the set pot might mean filling pails from the tap in the yard, or carrying water from the street tap. Florence Wood, born in 1914, a Blyth docker's daughter, remembers her mother carrying buckets of water up the two flights of stairs to their top floor flat.

For countrywomen, wash day could mean several trips to the village pump, the well or the spring, carrying the pails

hooked to the 'gerrit', a wooden framed contrivance which fitted round the waist. The device was called a 'gird', 'girth' or 'girdle' in different parts of the county. Mrs Elizabeth Ann Luck, a hind's daughter, born in 1912 at Whittonstall, recalls the hardness of the local spring water when they lived at Linzford in County Durham, and how her mother preferred to rely on rainwater barrels. 'If we'd have a dry spell, she'd have to use the spring water and, poor soul, it would take ages to get up a lather from the soap.'

The set pot filled, the fire was lit beneath it to heat the water. Sheets, towels, and linen previously left to soak could now be lifted on to the bench for scrubbing. Soap came in the form of solid, yellow blocks and the flakes had to be grated from it – there were no detergents at the time.

Florence Wood remembers: 'On windy days, the wives would have a real problem – either the fire would blow out, or it would roar up – they'd have to watch they didn't get their behinds scorched while they were busy scrubbing and rubbing on the washboard.' (A washboard was a wooden frame with a corrugated metal surface used to help rub away bad stains).

Once boiled, the laundry had to be lifted out of the set pot and into the deep (Belfast) sink and rinsed thoroughly in cold water to remove the remaining soap. It was then 'blued' (rinsed with a blue wash called 'Reckitts' Blue') to enhance the whiteness, before being put through the mangle to remove surplus water. This was all extremely hard, physical labour. Wet, cotton sheets are very heavy to lift and it needed more than a fair amount of muscle power to put a quarter-folded twill sheet through the mangle to squeeze out the water. Shirts – heavy cotton or cotton twill, not modern light polyester mixes – might also need cold-water starching before they could be put through the wringer and the rollers would then need rinsing to remove the sticky starch

Washday c.1910. The girls are using poss-sticks in a poss tub to agitate the dirty clothes.

before wringing anything else. The starching gave the shirts a crispness and helped to prevent dirt settling on the fabric.

Nowadays, we tend to look back critically at how seldom outer clothes were washed, but skirts, trousers, cardigans and jumpers were made from wool. Natural wool shrinks when it is washed. There were no man-made fibres, easily laundered

and dried; moreover, clothes were expensive to buy and had to be treated with great care.

Clean laundry was hung out to dry on the washing line, but the problems were not yet over. Washing had to be finely judged. If the fabric was allowed to become too dry it was impossible to iron with the flat iron heated on the fire. There were no electric irons then – the woman spat on the flatiron and if the saliva sizzled, the iron was hot enough. On the other hand, if the washing remained too damp, mildew was likely to ruin the garment or linen. A 'good drying day' meant light winds and temperatures around about 16-18° C. Winter drying was a great problem, for clothes froze on the line and the ice simply melted in the indoor heat. Women in the pit villages had the added anxiety and exasperation of having to take everything off the lines strung across the back lanes to allow access for the 'tankies' – the coal wagons which delivered heaps of concessionary coal to the pitmen – which then disgorged their dusty, black heaps in the lanes outside the houses.

'Eh, it used to make the women hopping mad. They'd been up afore dawn, scrubbing and pounding, so as to get the sheets out by nine-o-clock in the morning – and, by, there was great competition to be the first – and they'd just be clearing up, ready to get on with the rest of their jobs when they'd hear the shout, "Coal-ho!" Well out they'd rush to gather in the sheets and what-nots from the lines in armfuls – the smalls, mind you, were always hung in the back yard, it wasn't considered decent to show them off to everyone – anyway, they'd all be helping one another, then they'd have to untie the lines and wait until the whole lot could go up again when the tankie had gone. Ee, and whoever was getting the coal would be right embarrassed, even though it wasn't their fault.' (Florence Wood)

Mondays and Thursdays were also baking days – usually only bread was made on Monday, but Thursday was the day the children loved most for this was the day for baking scones, cakes, biscuits, lardy cake and granny loaf. Always anxious to get home from school quickly on a Thursday, the

Girdle Cake (Singin' Hinny)

1lb (450g) flour
$\frac{1}{2}$ tsp cream of tartar
$\frac{1}{4}$ tsp bicarbonate of soda
4oz (125g) lard
6oz (175g) currants
milk

Rub dry ingredients with the fats until the mixture resembles dry breadcrumbs. Stir in the currants. Add sufficient milk to make a dough. Roll out on a floured board to about a $\frac{1}{4}$ inch thick. Cook in the piece or shape into several smaller pieces. Cook on a traditional girdle, or use a heavy based frying pan, or cook in the oven. If you are cooking in the oven it will take about 20 minutes at 200°C (400°F Gas mark 6).
The above recipe is just a guide and it is possible to use self raising flour and dispense with the bicarbonate of soda and cream of tartar, or to use plain flour and 2 tsps baking powder. Some people use a mixture of milk and sour cream.

children looked out for the special treat which was usually put out on the kitchen window ledge to cool down. For some it was a bread bun, fresh from the oven, eaten with butter or home-made jam, for others it was lardy cake – bread dough baked with extra butter and sugar, then filled with currants.

Everyone remembers baking days with huge enthusiasm. Elizabeth Ann Luck describes the twice-weekly event:

'Mother had this huge earthenware mixing bowl – shiny brown on the outside and dull cream on the inside. She'd put in a stone [14lbs or 5kg] of flour, salt, yeast mixed with warm milk and water and a little fat. Then she'd mix it all up into a dough and work it. Her arms would be covered in flour and I still remember how muscular and strong they always looked as she squeezed and stretched the dough. Then she'd put the whole lot back into the bowl, cover it with a damp cloth, and put the bowl to the side of the black-leaded range for the dough to rise. Woebetide any child who slammed a door and caused a cold draught while the bread was rising! When it was proved, she'd tip it onto the big, wooden baking board, slice it into pieces and shape it into six two-pound loaf tins and prick each loaf with a fork. Back again to prove once more and then into a really hot oven to cook. We got lardy cake for our special treat on a Thursday, but we usually had rock cakes and scones then too. Believe me, nothing has ever tasted as good as Mam's home-made bread and cakes.'

'It was the heat,' explains Bert Robson born in 1907 in Whitley Bay, a plumber's son. 'They'd keep the "chiggies" (small coals) for the fire on baking days which produced a really steady, high temperature. Modern ovens can't get that intensity and, my goodness, it made such a difference. Yorkshire puddings as light as angels' wings; they melted on wor tongues. The bread managed to have a chewy and crispy crust but to be spongy and light inside – not like the flannelly stuff we buy from the shops nowadays – it had texture and taste. I tell you, if you haven't tasted food cooked in an old-fashioned oven, you can't claim to have lived.'

Food was almost invariably home-cooked and, in the country, mostly home-grown too. Hinds and shepherds always kept a pig and the wives home-cured the hams and bacon; they also made sausages, brawn, black and white puddings, for as everyone knew, you could eat all of the pig, except its squeak.

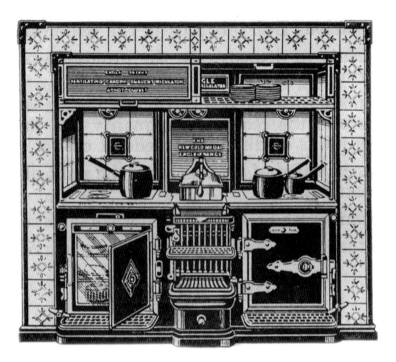

A state of the art kitchen range, 1923.

And some more basic rural kitchen arrangements, 1910.

Drop scones

4oz (125g) self-raising flour
1oz (25g) margarine
1 egg beaten with 5 or 6 tbsps (80-90ml) milk
2oz (50g) sugar
6 drops lemon juice
1/4 tsp salt

Mix flour and salt together and rub in margarine. Add the sugar and then smooth batter with the egg and milk. Add the lemon juice. Drop spoonfuls onto a hot girdle or frying pan. When the bubble bursts on the top of the scone turn it over to cook the other side. You can cook 2 or 3 at the same time.

Barley bread was a popular accompaniment to the bacon and new-laid eggs. Mrs Florence Dunn, born in 1909, a shepherd's daughter from Kidlandlee remembers the baking:

'Tom's [her husband's] family lived at East Wilkwood, miles away from anywhere – it's in the middle of the Army's Otterburn shooting ranges now – and sometimes the minister would have a walk out from Harbottle to see them. It was a real treat for his mother to have a visitor because they were so isolated. His father and all six lads were shepherds, so they were away in the hills all day. When the minister came, she'd make this enormous Singin' Hinny [a type of girdle scone], boil some fresh eggs and serve them with barley bread, home-made cheese and home-made jam. I miss barley bread, but you just cannot get it, nor the flour, nowadays.'

Rob McKenna from Coldrife says, 'We ate lots of home-made broths, packed with the vegetables which father grew in the garden. He'd leeks, onions, carrots, cabbages, peas, beans, turnips and beetroot. Sometimes, as I got a bit older, I'd gan oot and get a rabbit wi' my catapult and that would go in the stewpot.'

May Telfer recalls: 'We ate food according to the season then – no pork unless there was an R in the month. Soups, stews, all thick and nutritious. Mother would put the yetlin [a large, cast iron cooking pot] on the range in the morning and the meal would simmer gently all day. In the summer, there'd be lots of pies made with gooseberries or plums, blackcurrants or apples, and any amount of rhubarb. Much of the fruit was made into jams and preserves. Every good housewife spent much of the summer bottling or jam-making; pantries would be packed with kilner jars – a treasure trove of fruit and pickles.'

Broth

Bacon bone, ham shank, a pound of lap or anything to hand
2 large carrots
2 large parsnips
1 small turnip or half a large one
1 large leek
a couple of handfuls of split peas or lentils

Place bones, ham shank or whatever in a large pan and fill with cold water. Bring to the boil and then simmer until the meat is tender. Skim. Remove the meat. Dice the vegetables and add to the liquid. Bring to the boil again. Add lentils or split peas and simmer until all is cooked. Simmer until the thickness is to your liking. Meat may be chopped up and added to the broth or used for other purposes.

Not everything could be homegrown: tea, sugar and flour had to be bought. For the families of shepherds living in the isolated Cheviots, shopping required special arrangements.

In his very strong Northumbrian accent, complete with the fast-disappearing 'growling r', Tom Dunn, born in 1907, a shepherd's son who grew up in the lonely reaches of the Cheviot Hills at East Wilkwood, explained the system to me: 'They'd bring the stuff up by horse and cart in a box to Linbriggs and leave it there for you to collect. You put out a note saying what you needed for the next delivery and you'd make payment for the last one. They'd all be put under a stone for safety. Sometimes, mind you, you'd be snowed in and wouldn't be able to get down there to Linbriggs: in the winter of 1947-48 we were snowed in for thirteen weeks.

'I remember the Laidlers lived at Buckham Walls then – right away from anywhere, no place, just a little cottage – and in winter time they'd have to collect their stuff from Linn Burn. Noo he couldn't take his tea without sugar and they'd run oot, so he said, "Noo, mother, [his wife, that is, not his mother] if there's anything you want

from they groceries doon at Linn Burn, I'm gannin' doon t'get some things." Eh, he was that desperate for his sugar. He struggled doon there, and there was a good bit of snow around, mind you, an' he struggled back through it, the sack slung across his shoulders. His wife made a cup o' tea, and he slit the sack all ready to spoon sugar into his cup – it was then he discovered he'd brought back a sack of ground rice!

'I remember, too, that same winter, John Glendinning carrying a ten-stone sack of flour on his back in really deep

The isolation of the remote Cheviot farms in the early 20th century and in bad weather meant food might be very scarce in winter months. This is Sourhope farm.

snow, and he carried it the two miles from Blindburn to Makinton.'

Mr Laidler at Buckham Walls lived 1300 ft (500m) way up in the Cheviot Hills. The trek down to Linn Burn at 750ft (200m) is around 13 miles (15km); therefore, he struggled 26 miles (30 km), in extremely deep snow to bring back his sack of 'sugar'. Blindburn is roughly three miles east of Buckham Walls.

While busy mothers laundered, baked, washed down the furniture with vinegar and water, changed the straw bedding, scrubbed floors, beat mats and kept the household going, they were secure in the knowledge that their children could roam the local fields without harm.

'We'd take a bent pin and go up to the Pin Well where we believed that if you threw the pin over your shoulder into the well, your wish would come true. Often there'd be a tramp resting there and they'd tell us stories of where they'd been and what they'd seen. I'm sure that some of the stories were outrageously exaggerated, but they fascinated us. Eventually they'd say, "Now you get along home before your Mammy gets worried about where you are."' (Mildred Wright of Wooler)

May Douglas, whose father was a hind in Bamburgh, says, 'The castle was our playground. There were no keys in those days, no need for them. We used to go there and run through the corridors. There were stone flags down and we loved the sound of our footsteps on them. Then we'd go up to the Keep, where the big well was and drop pebbles down it until you heard them splash. We all firmly believed the story

Bamburgh Castle c.1910.

of the Laidley Worm and the Princess.'

Rob McKenna recalls searching the hills of Simonside looking for fairy rings, 'Eh, I'd be eleven or twelve then. But we were so innocent then.'

Mrs Sparke (born in 1914, from Keenley in West Allendale) recalls: 'In the summer, we'd take jam sandwiches, a bottle of water and we'd all go off to the fields and woods to play all day. Mind you, we had to be home by eight or there was trouble. It was always easier for the boys to get away, most of the girls had jobs to do, or younger children to take care of, so it wasn't as easy for them. From an early age we were taught to knit and darn and mend and, in a large family, there was always plenty of mending.'

All around were sights and scents to delight. There were road-menders, with steaming vats of pitch and heaps of stones, mending potholes in the roads. There were gigs, phaetons, traps, landaus, carriages and carts – all as familiar to children then as various makes of car are to today's children.

Horses played a crucial and pungent part in the lives of these children, for where there are horses, there are also smiths and smithies – a source of endless fascination.

'We used to love watching them put the rims on cart wheels with that special tool they had [an adze]. Or to see them making shoes, with sparks flying everywhere and that peculiar smell, like singed hair, when the shoe is fitted to the horse's hoof. If we were very lucky, we might even be allowed to work the

bellows.' (May Telfer)

Mrs Bolam, born 1912, the daughter of an Alnwick solicitor, was brought up in a much more affluent household. 'We were really quite poor. Mother had only one live-in maid, a daily help and a woman who came in to do the laundry. She had to do her own cooking. My grandmother, however, was much more well-to-do: she had three live-in maids, a house-

Farm carts were the usual way of transporting goods and people.

20

keeper and a cook.' Mrs Bolam's childhood was considerably more circumscribed than that of her poorer, but freer contemporaries. Lady-like walks were taken with Miss Amos, her governess; or with a maid. In winter, the nursery was her playground; in it were her doll's house, china tea sets, rocking horse and many other toys. In summer she played in the large garden. The companionship of other children was provided on a more formal basis when the children of her parents' friends visited. This was the stable, orderly childhood considered eminently suitable for an Edwardian middle-class child. It lacked the freedom and social interaction enjoyed by the poorer children, but life would soon redress the balance. While Mrs Bolam's social freedom would increase, that of her poorer contemporaries, compelled to earn their own living, would became narrower and narrower.

A more affluent family might even have its own carriage and coachman.

Adam's ale

'You dursen't dare cry no matter how cold it was.'

Water was rarely on tap inside the house, especially in the countryside. As children of more affluent parents, Mrs Bolam, Alice Sanderson (born in 1900, an Alnwick policeman's daughter), Minnie Craighead (born in Tynemouth in 1912, her father a superintendent engineer), Mrs Buglass (grand daughter of a Sanitary Inspector), and Mildred Wright (daughter of a bank manager), all grew up in homes with hot and cold running water, and with bathrooms.

Mrs Turnbull's father, an enterprising man, was a master shaft sinker at a small colliery in Melkridge, south Tynedale. Having seen pictures in magazines of bathrooms, he decided that his own home should have one. He built a room onto the back of the house in which he placed a full-size bath, which stood on heavy, clawed feet. Unfortunately, he didn't understand plumbing and the bath had to be filled manually with hot water from the kitchen range. It was emptied into the garden through a hose.

In the countryside water was usually carried in buckets from a nearby source; a village pump, a street tap or a spring using the 'ger-

An earth closet, used in houses with no plumbing.

rit' to stop water spilling from the pails *en route*. Occasionally, the water source was some distance away from the house. Carrying water from its source was often the first and last chore of the day for the older children of the household.

Christopher Blandford, born in 1920, whose father was a miner, but whose mother belonged to the fisherfolk, describes what happened in Newbiggin: 'We lived in a stone cottage on Main Street. There was one cold tap outside for each row – five cottages on one side and six on the other. On winter mornings, straw was packed round the tap and set on fire to unfreeze the pipe. Most folks, though, had a rain barrel and I well recall my grandfather cutting my hair. He'd dunk my whole

B. Denness

The village pump in Allendale.

22

head into the barrel – ice notwithstanding – before taking up the scissors. In those days we had to be tough, you dursen't dare cry, no matter how cold it was.'

Mrs Cox, born in 1905, also in Newbiggin, lived in a flat above her father's small shop. Their outside tap frequently refused to give any water and they'd have to use the village pump or the spring at Church Point. Elizabeth Ann Luck of Whittonstall, remembers the tap outside the kitchen which brought such hard water from the local spring.

In Ashington, frozen street taps forced the boys to be sharp-witted. Jimmy Ditchburn whose gardener father had died of peritonitis, remembers: 'We had two taps out in the lane, but if ours were frozen we'd have to seek water from somebody else's and that wasn't always that easy, especially if the lads in the next street were a rival gang. In that case, you needed guile. You'd get something to distract them while a couple of others nipped in, filled the buckets and carried them away – all without spilling a drop mind. I've had many a split lip from fighting over the taps.'

Water shortages caused by long, dry summers and mild winters are not a new phenomenon. While today's shortages might mean a hosepipe ban, in those days droughts posed a very real health hazard. Among other things, hot weather brought outbreaks of the dreaded 'infantile paralysis' now known as poliomyelitis.

Mrs Buglass's grandfather was the Sanitary Inspector in Berwick; part of his duties involved inspecting water sources,

A water pant in Sele Park, Hexham, around 1910.

especially those of farms.

'He would go round with Dr Heagarty, the Medical Officer of Health. But to indicate to you of how little importance the Council thought that task to be, the two men had to hire and pay for their own pony and trap to do the job. They borrowed some dynamite from the quarry once and blew up a pump in Spittal because it was causing cholera and the Council would do nothing. I remember them laughing about it. When I read a very similar incident in a novel by A.J. Cronin, I was quite put out because it was grandfather's and Dr Heagarty's story.'

It was not until 1929 that legislation was passed empowering County Councils to make grants towards the cost of rural water schemes. Until then, Water Boards were entirely privately-subscribed and, as such, preferred large numbers of customers in a relatively compact, geographical area. Rural schemes tended to be rare, and work on providing safe reservoir supplies was sporadic. The long, hot summer of 1932 brought matters to crisis point. Throughout the county, villagers found their springs and wells drying up and there was alarm as they were left with only contaminated pools and depleted wells. Without adequate water supplies, dairy farmers, in particular, found it increasingly difficult to maintain adequate hygiene amongst the herds. It seemed that no one had records of from where or how rural populations obtained water. At this point, the Northumberland Federation of Women's Institutes took up the cudgels on behalf of its members and country-dwellers. Each Institute was asked to take part in a county-wide water survey and to appoint a 'Water Secretary' to collate local results. With impressive efficiency, members reported back on the supply situation for every household in their district. The results were then forwarded to the County Federation, which put together all the findings and sent them to the County Council. A huge amount of work was involved in the survey, the scope and accuracy of the data could not be denied and the authorities could no longer ignore the problem.

Hard as it is to imagine, inadequate or contaminated water supplies remained a contentious issue until well into the first half of the 20th century. In Morpeth, there was an outbreak of typhoid in the area of Back Riggs, immediately behind the town centre, as late as 1936. The town was a warren of alleys, open cesspits and decrepit, cheap lodging houses (often owned by Town Councillors). Morpethians had complained for years about the state of Back Riggs and the stink emanating from it. It took the typhoid outbreak to force the Council to demolish the overcrowded, insanitary Victorian slums.

Infectious diseases were a constant threat to families. Having survived their infancies, the contributors to this book then had to face the other health hazards of the time: diphtheria, tuberculosis, poliomyelitis, measles, whooping cough, scarlet fever, mumps, chicken pox, rubella and, not least of all, the great danger of wounds turning septic and blood-poisoning setting in.

Alice Sanderson was diagnosed as having 'tubercular glands' from infected milk (pasteurisation eventually became

The prize winner in a 'Clean Milk' competition organised by Northumberland County Council, September 1926.

compulsory in order to avoid bovine tubercular infection). Two sisters who lived nearby had recently died of TB and when Alice and her brother began to sicken, their parents promptly sought medical help. A specialist from the Royal Victoria Infirmary, Newcastle upon Tyne, was finally persuaded to operate on the two children. One Saturday morning he turned up at the house in order to perform the operation. Mrs Sanderson's mother had scrubbed down the kitchen table until it gleamed almost white. Before the eminent specialist would remove the infected glands, her father had to count out twenty golden sovereigns onto the table. Alice says she still remembers the pile of gold and the stench of the chloroform the surgeon used to anaesthetise her and her brother.

Maggie Brown, born in 1898, a fisherman's daughter from Newbiggin, remembers having diphtheria and being extremely ill. To the surprise of the family, her brother, who had always been considered rather sickly, missed being infected.

Sally H., a hind's daughter from Chathill, is proud of having been a fit child but recalls clearly how upset her brother was on having to miss Wooler Show because he'd gone down with measles.

As always, the British obsession with bowels meant the children were frequently dosed with purgatives. Certainly, the Spring

Benger's food was just one of a number of trusted home remedies.

Purge – to cleanse the blood of its winter impurities, not unlike the present fashion for 'detoxification' – seems to have been important to all parents. Syrup of Figs, syrup and sulphur, castor oil, cascara, prunes and other purgatives were given to children every March; some were even dosed on a weekly basis throughout the year.

May Telfer gives the recipe which her North Sunderland/Seahouses grandfather boiled up for the family to ease chesty coughs: 'You need linseed oil, water, a big bar of licquorice, vinegar and a wee bit of sugar. You boil it all up in the yetlin [cast iron cauldron] until it is syrupy, then you leave it to cool and bottle it.'

She also recalls their family doctor, Dr McClaskey of Bamburgh, whose surgery above the Bamburgh Castle Hotel had the text of 'Lead, Kindly Light' on one wall. 'The Doctor originally had a pony and trap but eventually he got himself one of those little mopeds, you know, the pedal cycles with a motor on them? When he got it, he pushed it along the road trying to make it go and it wouldn't. So, in the end, he took it back to Tom at the garage and complained. Then Tom said to him, "Did you never think of putting a bit petrol into it, Doctor?"'

May also tells the tale of a fisher lad who had a constant need for castor oil. 'Well, when he came back for the fourth bottle in a month, Dr McClaskey began to get a bit worried and he says to him, "You know, Ned. If you've such a problem with your bowels, perhaps we'd better get the hospital to take a look at you." Well, Ned was really panicked at that and he said, "There's nothing wrong wi' me nor with me bowels, Doctor, it's just me father says the castor oil is grand for waterproofing his boots.'"

For the pitmen, 6d a week ensured comprehensive health care for them and their families for it meant that they were on the Doctor's panel and could call him – invariably a 'him' in those days – whenever he was needed. This could be a great relief in a difficult childbirth, especially as babies were almost always delivered at home. But there were other reasons for calling out the doctor and May Telfer, for instance, attributes her brother Arthur's life to Bamburgh's Dr McClaskey who saved him during a particularly virulent bout of measles.

Others fondly recall the kindness of both Drs Cluckvin – father and son – in Alnwick.

Doctors, though, were generally called as a last resort, when all home remedies had failed, or when serious illness was suspected. For everyone, the greatest fear of all was that of contracting TB (also known as consumption), for which there was then no cure. After that, perhaps septicaemia was the biggest threat. Without antibiotics, inflammations could spread rapidly and maim or kill. All the old people remembered having scraped knees washed with disinfectant, or the sting of iodine being painted on to prevent infection. For some there was the misery of boils and carbuncles and the extremely hot dressings intended to 'draw' the poison out. They remember hot kaolin bandages or bread poultices for chesty colds. Then there were the embarrassing skin infestations like scabies, impetigo and ringworm where 'gentian blue' or 'vermilion' was painted over all of the infected area, promptly identifying those who'd been affected and making them instantly the butt of everyone's scorn. Ringworm was frequently contracted from contact with infected cattle and had little to do with cleanliness. Less serious, but just as embarrassing, was nit infestation, which mothers dreaded because it (quite unjustly) raised questions about family hygiene practices. In some cases, I'm sure that children survived in spite of, rather than because of, the home remedies administered to them.

Miss Frances Lamb, born in 1900, a pitman's daughter from Redburn, near Bardon Mill in Tynedale, tells of the time she and her sister contracted whooping cough. 'Nothing would shift it, so Daddy got permission to take us into Barcombe Pit because he believed that the chemicals from the coal would do us good. Well it must have done something, because I'm 102 and still going strong.'

The Great War

'Poor fellow. He lost his wife and his son within the year.'

Events of the First World War are often amongst the earliest recollections of contributors. At only two years old, Mrs Bolam was lifted to the window to watch her young uncle march down the drive away from the house. 'Remember this moment,' her mother urged, 'for you may never see him again.' These were prophetic words: Mrs Bolam does not recall her uncle ever returning to Alnwick after he went off to war. He was killed in action in 1917.

Minnie Craighead could never understand why the gas lights on the streets of her hometown of Tynemouth were dimmed when the steel works at Jarrow, just across the Tyne, were lit up like a guiding beacon. The precautions did not stop air raids. 'Zeppelins came in over the river, which was very frightening.' But there were some good times and Minnie remembers her 15 minutes of wartime fame. 'My mother held a sale of work in our back yard to raise money for comforts – dried fruits, sweets and cigarettes – for the troops. She worked with the Red Cross and had got me a little uniform, which I insisted on wearing during the sale. The local paper then had a photo of me, in my uniform, with the headline, "Little Miss Small". I've always regretted that I lost it somewhere when I moved.

'I remember that all the ships' hooters on the Tyne were blown on Armistice Day. I must have been sick, for I remem-

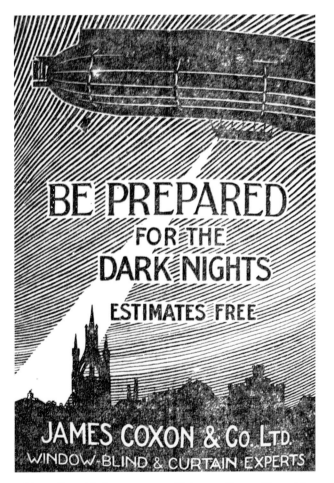

Zeppelin raids became a terrifying reality on Tyneside.

27

ber Mother sitting on my bed and crying her eyes out because her brothers would now come home.'

Bob Duff, from North Shields, also remembers the zeppelins and searchlights above the river: 'Mother was always anxious. Father was then the chief skipper of a minesweeper which was based in the Albert Edward Dock, North Shields. The zeppelins used to lay mines and then the minesweepers went out to search for them. It was a hazardous job and I can understand now why she was always in such a state of anxiety.'

Rob McKenna of Coldrife, near Rothbury, was at school when the war broke out. 'Our headmaster was Charles Hinley Cook, and he went off to war. A Mr Brewer came to take his place and his son joined the Flying Corps – later to become the RAF. I remember we were all taken out into the playground to wave goodbye as his son marched off to Fontburn station. Mr Brewer rushed off to wave to the train. I can see him waving now. Poor fellow. He lost his son and his wife within the year. The old boy used to have a St John's Ambulance uniform and it was always greasy with bacon

fat and the like. He'd no idea how to care for himself. Or perhaps he didn't care.'

Olive Purves, born in 1905, whose father was a tobacconist in Wooler, was the youngest of seven children; she lost her eldest brother, 'He lived in Blyth. He was married and had a small son. Another brother survived though. He went down to Manchester after the war and served his time at Westinghouse [a large engineering works]. Eventually, he went to Mexico and married there. I still keep in touch with his family.'

The departure of the Sixth Northumberland Fusiliers for France, April 1915.

For Mildred Wright Peace Day in 1918 was a big day, 'We had a procession to Humbleton Hill, Wooler. All the children were in fancy dress and my sister was dressed as a Kate Greenaway character [Kate Greenaway was a well-known illustrator of children's stories. Her children are all cherubic and cute]. She sat in a little cart which I pulled. There was a big picnic afterwards, with lots of food.'

Florence Wood of Blyth, was born after her dock worker father had left for the war. When he returned she was afraid of this strange man who made her mother laugh and weep at the same time, 'He wore puttees and looked very strange. I cried and made an awful fuss when I saw him.'

May Telfer was eleven years old. She remembers an immediate family catastrophe when war was declared. Each year, German ships would sit at anchor just off her home village of North Sunderland and Seahouses, ready to take on board the barrels of salted and smoked herring which were rowed out to them. This was an extremely important and lucrative trade on the coast, and I'll say more about it later. Mrs Telfer's uncle owned a smokery/saltery and all his summer output in 1914 was sold to the Germans. The barrels were delivered to the waiting vessels, which steamed away, as usual, in late July. War was declared on August 3rd and the bill for the herring was never paid. Mrs Telfer's uncle was pushed right to the edge of bankruptcy, an extremely serious situation at that time. Similar financial catastrophes must have happened in all of the fishing communities from the far north of Scotland to Great Yarmouth in Suffolk, all of whom relied on the

A Victory tea party, probably Spring 1919.

herring trade which was never to be the same again.

The odd thing is, that despite two World Wars, a General Strike and a long economic Depression, the contributors, more often than not, remember happy childhoods. How resilient we humans are.

Happiest days

'I recall my first day at school, I walked three miles to get there.'

Twins Margaret and Issie Douglas. Margaret was sent to the Duchess School, Alnwick.

In Northumberland, hinds were employed on an annual contract which ran from May 12th to May 11th each year. May 12th was 'Flitting Day'. This meant that the children of hinds often attended a different school each year or returned to one they'd attended some years before.

Very few children took examinations, although a few do remember the 'Grading Exam' which they sat at eleven years of age. Children who were successful were, in theory at least, eligible to go to grammar school. Often, however, children who passed the exam were unable to take up their grammar school place, simply because family finances could not bear the cost of travel and the equipment needed by a scholar. On the whole, clever girls fared even less well than their brothers, partly because of the prevailing belief that education was likely to be wasted on a girl who would get married, rather than pursuing a career; but also for the simple reason that there were far fewer county grammar school places available for girls than boys. In either respect, things did not improve much for female pupils until after World War Two. Margaret Douglas though, was one of twin daughters born to an Amble miner and his dressmaker wife. The twin girls were their only children, so Margaret was able to take up her scholarship to Duchess School, Alnwick; she later became a teacher. She remembers the chaos of schooling during the Great War, 'Because of the war school was held in the Middlemass' house. Lady Victoria Percy had grabbed the school as a Red Cross Centre. We had to take our lessons all over the town – the Northumberland Hall, for instance, and the Guildhall.'

For most of the elderly contributors (excluding the hinds' children mentioned earlier) the whole of their educational experience was within one, local school. Starting at the local Elementary aged five, they went on from class to class until they reached twelve or fourteen, depending on the statutory leaving age. Before 1919, this was twelve then it rose to fourteen.

Sally H., born in the north of the county at Chathill,

close to Seahouses: 'I recall my first day at school. I walked three mile to get there. It was early September and I'd be just a few days after my fifth birthday. I can remember being so proud of the new dress Mother had made, and I wore a new, white pinafore over it, which had lace around the yoke. I had on home-knitted, black stockings and fresh garters, made with elastic, and laced boots on my feet. Eh, but my legs ached when I arrived. You soon got used to it though, and there'd be lots of others going, so the distance just flew by when you were with your friends.'

Tynemouth c.1910.

Mrs Betty Robson, born in Netherwitton, in 1903, was the daughter of a coachman. The family moved to Tynemouth when she was four and she attended Tynemouth Priory School. Miss Tyson was her teacher in Class 3 and Miss Pigg in Class 4. A clever needlewoman, Betty won a number of school prizes for her sewing. She was most proud of a nightdress 'feather-stitched and pleated, it was made from a length of white cotton.' Her teacher referred to this material as 'nainsnook'.

'I also enjoyed learning poetry and remember reading *Midsummer Night's Dream* and a poem which began, "Beautiful Evelyn Hope is dead". [*Evelyn Hope* by Robert Browning]. There was also another one called *Lady Clare* [Tennyson] and *The Slave's Dream* [H.W. Longfellow]. They were also very keen on concerts and singing at Tynemouth Priory School.'

Minnie Craighead whose father was a Superintendent Engineer for Richard Irvine and Sons, also attended school in Tynemouth at a private Dame's School run by a very old lady and her daughter. 'The old lady always wore a long gown and a white lace cap on her head. Even in summer, the girls were expected to wear white gloves and felt, or straw, hats when out of doors … the school curriculum was restricted to English, arithmetic and embroidery.'

The latter subject was, in her mother's opinion, a great mistake, since Minnie left school having never learned to turn a hem or sew on a button properly. All the same, Minnie felt that she had had an 'excellent grounding'. She remembers that the Dame's daughter was extremely fond of Tennyson's poems, but they did no Shakespeare. 'All the same, *The Wreck of the Hesperus* would move me to tears.' Apart from school, there were also dancing lessons and music lessons. Minnie admits, 'I was an only and much-cossetted child.'

Girls at Elswick school, Newcastle, 1914.

School hours for Minnie were 10 a.m. to 12 noon and 1.30 p.m. until 4 p.m. Having an hour and a half for lunch, she was able to go home.

More usually, state school pupils began at 9 a.m. and finished at 4 p.m., although, in winter, when it got dark by 4 p.m., schools would finish at 3.30 p.m. to allow country children, who often – like Sally at Chathill – walked long distances to school, to get home before darkness fell because there was no lighting on the roads. For lunch, the country pupils took sandwiches and a tin bottle of tea; the bottle was usually placed on top of the classroom stove to keep warm. Rob McKenna recalls, 'When [the tin bottles] got hot, the tops would often pop right out and interrupt the lesson'. He and his classmates preferred not tea, but Van Houten's cocoa to drink.

The curriculum in the elementary school would vary somewhat according to the teachers' interests. Most contributors report doing simple arithmetic; one or two went on to do algebra. History and geography were taught and pupils followed the battles of World War One. It was also an age when the sun never set on the British Empire; when most of the schoolroom globe was coloured pink to denote British imperial supremacy.

'You couldn't help it, you felt proud to be British' recalls Mr Price, born in 1900, a farmer's son from Newton by the Sea. Mrs Cassie, the Longhoughton hind's daughter, was also patriotic: 'I loved reading about famous battles, Nelson at Trafalgar, for instance. The men we read of were our heroes and we were proud to be British like them.' The first gramophone record Mrs Cassie ever heard was at school: it was a recording of King George V and Queen Mary making an Empire Day speech.

Olive Purves, born in Wooler, the youngest child of a tobacconist, liked school but hated Mr Leech, the schoolmaster, 'I had a reputation for being a bit of a handful, but I think I was quite good. I loved history.' Janet Robinson, born in 1898 at Haydon Bridge, recalled Miss Gibson at Shaftoe Trust School, 'She was little and fat and always knitting. If you misbehaved, she hit you with her needles.' In Lesbury, where May Robson, a railwayman's daughter born in Newcastle in 1905, went to school, the female pupils loved the way in which their two female teachers (sisters) were dressed, but were suspicious about the too tidy hair of one and were convinced that she wore a wig. In Red Row, close to Broomhill, and just inland from Druridge Bay, Ned Thompson, born in 1918, and others sang the praises of Mr Jackson, the headteacher. 'He kept pushing us to get the best out of us. He wasn't satisfied just to let us go. Oh, no, not he. Red Row School performed Shakespeare plays for the parents. We had a prize-winning garden too. Mr Jackson got us to plan it out, dig into the thick clay, improve it with manure and plant.

Then, when the plants grew, we also had a bit of botany, so we could recognise the things we were growing.'

Ned also pointed out the speed with which the School Board Man would visit, should a pupil be absent. 'Honestly, nowadays they can truant for months on end, but if we had even just half a day, he'd be on our doorstep wanting to know what was wrong with us and why we weren't at school. Then all the neighbours would know the School Board Man had been to see us and would gossip about it and our parents would be ashamed.'

Tom Dunn, a Cheviot shepherd's son, never had the opportunity to attend school. Way out in the middle of Cheviot, his existence appears to have been overlooked by the Education Authority (given the way farming employment worked, it isn't surprising that a youngster could disappear

Longhoughton schoolhouse.

33

from the statistics). As the youngest in the family, he simply followed his father and brothers around the hills. His skill with his flocks became legendary amongst other shepherds until, eventually, the Department of Agriculture at Kings College, Newcastle (then part of Durham University) heard of it and sent a group of researchers to find out whether what they had heard was true. Several flocks were put together in one field and Tommy was asked to count the sheep. This he did in just a couple of minutes. The four researchers took half an hour to confirm his count (which was, of course, absolutely accurate). Tom was then asked to identify which of the unmarked sheep belonged to which owners. Again, within just a few minutes, he and his collie had sorted out and penned the flocks, without a single mistake. Tom found it entirely puzzling that the University people thought his skill unusual, 'I've been round sheep all me life. Why wouldn't I know one from t'other?'

Looking after the sheep, a lonely rural job, c.1930.

In some parts of the county, schools celebrated special days. In Bamburgh, for instance, Lord Armstrong's birthday meant a day's holiday. In other places, custom required that the schoolmaster be shut out of the school in order to procure a holiday (Barring-out Day). Mrs Sparke remembers that this happened each Christmas at Keenley. The pupils would lock out the schoolteacher at lunchtime and demand to be released early for their Christmas holiday. All was fine, until someone forgot to tell the new schoolmistress who became extremely angry and threatened to beat the students within an inch of their lives unless they allowed her in.

Picture the children of the time: girls in white pinafores over a dark dress, laced boots on their feet and hand-knitted, black stockings, held up with home-made, elastic garters. Perhaps they wore a ribbon in their hair. Boys in knee-length shorts, sometimes cut down from father's former best trousers; laced boots, hand-knitted socks which came up to the knee (also held up with elastic), a hand-knitted jersey – usually with darned patches at the elbows, or slightly mismatched sleeves, re-knitted with the nearest matching colour when judged too thin to patch. Hair was often home-cut, using a pudding basin as a cutting guide.

At playtime, they might spill out of school into an asphalt playground; some were fortunate enough to be able to play in the surrounding fields. What were their games?

On concrete yards, girls could chalk out 'bays' for hopscotch. On asphalt, they did the same with a stick. School walls with high-set windows or, even better, boiler houses with none, provided areas on which to chalk goalposts for football or stumps for cricket. These areas also provided a hard surface against which girls could bounce their 'two balls'.

May Telfer remembers sitting under an oak which had been cleft by lightning in a field next to the school in North Sunderland. There, she and her friends played shops, with dock leaves for plates, pebbles for hard goods, and sand for sugar and flour. She also recalls making a set of scales from two boot polish tins and the metal support from beneath the leaf of the kitchen table. 'Mother never did find out where the support had gone.' She remembers 'Diablo' – two sticks with a ball to balance between them – being the craze for a while.

Girls whipped tops into a frenzy, boys rolled metal hoops. Tag, or 'Tiggy' as it was known in Northumberland was popular with both boys and girls, as was rounders. Skipping games though, were female territory along with all the many rhymes which went with them, such as:

Jelly on a plate
Jelly on a plate
Wibble-wobble, Wibble-wobble
Jelly on a plate
or
Sally go round the stars
Sally go round the moon
Sally go round the chimney pots
On a Sunday afternoon
or

Raspberry, strawberry, marmalade, jam
Tell me the name of your young man
or
I wrote a letter to my Love
And on the way I lost it
Somebody has picked it up and put it in their pocket

Girls also played numerous games holding hands and going round in circles: Ring a Ring a Roses, The Farmer Wants a Wife, Poor Sally is a-weeping, Rise Sally Walker.

As the girls skipped and juggled, the boys played marbles or leapfrog or leapt across another group lined up at a wall

Playtime around 1900. Nobody is without a hat. Lantern slide by photographer Edgar G. Lee.

in 'British Bulldog'. There were also the seasonal games such as conkers, cricket, football.

Inside the classroom, children were expected to be attentive, still, and obedient. They shared a double desk, often becoming firm friends with their desk partner. Beyond the infants' class, where they used slate and pencil, they used steel-nibbed pens and watery ink (made every Monday morning by the 'Ink Monitors' – a much-envied position which rewarded the well-behaved) to produce properly-spelt, beautifully-written pieces of work. Lack of attention, disobedience, blotty or careless work, all earned corporal punishment – the strap, belt or cane (or knitting needle at Shaftoe Trust School).

Frances Lamb of Redburn, remembers the awe in which the children held Mr Carroll, the headmaster of Henshaw School. She recounts a well-known village story about Mr Carroll which happened well before she was born.

'He went off to Scotland [the School Log indicates that he was on interview for another job] and had to change trains in Edinburgh when he realised that he'd left his coat behind on the first train. He went back to retrieve it and so missed the train to Dundee. That was the one which fell into the River Tay [on Sunday, 27 December 1879] when the railway bridge collapsed. Everyone in the village always said it was a really lucky escape, but even years later, when I went to school, all we children were really sorry that he'd missed that train. Oh, he was a tyrant. Always ready to use the strap. We were terrified of him. And if you went home and complained, you'd just get smacked again for being in trouble at school.'

For Mrs Sparke the problem was not in being at the Keenley school near Allendale, it was in getting there, for she

Small boys with improvised toys made from scraps.

had to cross a field in which there was a Leicester tup (a ram). 'He'd got his horns wrapped in rags, but I was only five years old and he'd be able to give me a nasty thump. But my father insisted that I should cross that field on my own and get over being frightened. I never did. As long as the tup was in that field, I was always terrified.'

Mrs Bolam (grand-daughter of the Middlemass family, whose home was used as part of the girls' grammar school during World War One) was taught by a governess and then, at eight years old, was sent to Queen Ethelburga's School in Harrogate. 'It was extremely strict, very High Church, and full of very rich girls whose fathers were in the woollen trade, so my mother wasn't at all happy about it. A friend of hers had a governess who'd attended Sherbourne School in Dorset and she recommended it highly, so my mother went down there to see. She must have liked what she saw, for the following September I began at Sherbourne School for Girls. I travelled by train to London, stayed overnight with an Aunt and then was taken to Waterloo to catch the school train. We had a train to ourselves, for we were quite a large school.

'Our daily routine was to rise at 7.30 a.m., breakfast at 8 a.m. and we were in school at 9 a.m. In winter we spent the evenings doing our homework, but during summer, some time was put aside for prep [homework] each afternoon and we had games in the evening. We played hockey, lacrosse, cricket and tennis. I don't remember being at all homesick. I think I must have known from the time I was quite small that I would go away to school, much as my elder brother had already done.

'At 18, after failing French in my Higher School Cert., I was sent to Paris. My mother had learnt of a family who took in English girls. Everything was in French. I certainly learned the language. I ended up dreaming in French. We went to lessons, museums, the ballet, the theatre and were very closely chaperoned. Madamoiselle taught us our lessons and we went to school or college to learn about French History and culture. I remember being taken on a tour of the chateaux of the Loire and the bus carrying us broke down. We found accommodation overnight, but were shocked at being expected to share double beds with our fellow pupils.'

Mildred Wright, was also sent to a private school. 'My sister went down with scarlet fever and the doctor recommended the clear air of Grassington, my mother's home area, for convalescence, so then we were both sent off to school in Harrogate, Yorkshire. We stayed at school until we were sixteen and then my mother felt that it was time for us to be at home to help her.'

Most pupils, though, left as soon as they were able to do so, clutching the Labour Certificate which allowed them to seek work.

The Education Act of 1918 raised the school-leaving age to 14. Before then it was possible to become a part-timer (attending school for half a day and work for the other half) or to leave school at 13, provided that statutory attendance had been completed.

Too soon, at an age which nowadays we regard as young adolescence, it was time for most youngsters get a job and begin to pull their financial weight in the household.

Hockey-players, 1931.

Village trades

'Ernie Hill boasted his shoes would last a lifetime.'

Even during the early part of the 20th century, some traditional crafts and trades were beginning to disappear from village life.

May Telfer remembers how many goods were transported and stored in barrels: 'The butter was in barrels, vinegar, bananas – little Canary ones which Mother mashed with raspberry jam, sugar and cream – they came in barrels; we had barrels of apples, even the grapes came in barrels. In North Sunderland, there were several coopers who did nothing but make barrels for the herring. They had this adze thing which they used to fit the hoops.'

Wooden barrels are rare nowadays. Even beer casks tend to be low-maintenance metal and the extraordinary skill of coopering has just about disappeared. Our language, too, has lost many of the words which recognised the importance of barrels. Few of us now would know the volume of a hogshead (approx 239 litres), a kilderkin (82 litres), or a firkin (41 litres).

Herrings being packed into barrels in North Sunderland around 1890.

A typical village at the beginning of the 20th century would almost certainly have its own blacksmith and farrier. There might also be coopers, millers, saddlers, shoemakers, milliners and dressmakers. Certainly in my own village of Redburn, Tynedale, in 1900, within 100 yards of where I now live, there was a butcher, a shoemaker, and a milliner; the blacksmith's shop was less than quarter of a mile away, and there was a hay rake maker and cartwright a mere half a mile away. None of these now exist and not a single one of my contributors took up employment in these traditional craft trades. Part of the reason for this was undoubtedly because craft skills were often passed down from father to son, or mother to daughter in the case of millinery. If a craftsman took on an apprentice, then he demanded a 'premium' because the apprentice would be relatively unproductive for a long time. Instruction, however, takes time and patience, which would inevitably slow down the crafts-man's own production rate. Few of my contributors' parents could afford the premium, or the low wages earned over the long apprenticeship period, often amounting to seven years.

Change, though, was already in the air. Whilst May Telfer's first job was to drive a delivery cart with genuine horse power, she had already seen her first motor vehicles.

'My Aunt Beanie had the first car I ever heard of, but she lived in the town [Newcastle]. A man with a red flag had to walk in front of the vehicle when she went out. My first proper sighting of a motor car was when Bob McKenzie, one

West Newcastle Local Studies

A new-fangled motor car at White House Farm, Northumberland, 1914.

of the directors of Newcastle United, came to the village [North Sunderland]. Word got round that he was in one of these new-fangled motor cars and all we children rushed to see it. I remember it had little spokey wheels, which might even have been wooden ones, and a big, canvas hood and he was sitting up high there in his leather helmet, goggles and gauntlets, pumping the horn.

'But I have to say that we were familiar with horses. Big draught horses were used for ploughing and the like; half-cobs, which were lighter horses, pulled the traps; and we had small, high-stepping horses for the gigs. My job used a short cart – it had pieces up the side and the backboard let-down.

You sat in the cart to drive it. You just got used to handling horses and learning about them. I couldn't have gone for my job at Lucker if I hadn't been handling them.'

Milk floats, dray wagons, coal carts and the horses which drew them remained a familiar sight in both town and country until the middle of the 20th century, their use well-extended, despite the internal combustion engine, by the Second World War and subsequent petrol shortages. Farriers and blacksmiths, although fewer in number, still had enough work to keep them going until the mid-1950s. Wheelwrights, however, were a disappearing breed. As roads improved, the need to replace wheels on carts and waggons (carts had two wheels, waggons had four) became much less frequent. The wheelwright's work had always been somewhat seasonal, for farmers rarely had their vehicles over-hauled until the spring. Winter was a time to prepare for the spring rush, to cut wood to the required shape and leave it to season. A good wheelwright pre-ferred to choose his own ash, oak, elm or beech from that felled during the dor-mant season. His choice of timber would be dictated by his customers' require-ments, and how the curve of the felled trees fitted his needs; this though, meant that a considerable amount of profit was tied up in stocked timber. Spokes, for example, were made of heart of oak which was split green and left to season for some years before being shaped as required. By the end of World War Two,

his trade was fast disappearing.

The village smith survived a little longer and he had to be a versatile man since every job which required metal-working came to him. At Tow House, near Bardon Mill in Tynedale, the village blacksmiths for most of the 19th century were the Hardings and in the blacksmith's books still in the possession of Ruth Forster – a descendant of John Harding – there are accounts of work being done on harrows, hacks, coulters, girds, turnip hoes, colrakes, grubbers and heamsticks. Axles were repaired; plough irons, scuffling shears, forks, axes, chisels, hoes, plough shares and coulters were sharpened; hammers were rolled and steeled, and bridles mended. In

A rest for the horse after a ploughing match around 1930.

addition to these tasks, the blacksmith was regularly employed in making gates, or in repairing chains, locks and window clasps and fashioning new snecks and bolts for doors. Small, domestic repairs were also undertaken such as the mending and making of fire grates, or the sealing of holes in the precious cast iron pots and pans which people expected to last them a lifetime. In reading the blacksmith's account books (copies of which can be seen at Northumberland County Archives), there is a strong sense of the blacksmith's shop being the centre of village life. Frequently, one can trace a sudden run of small repairs being requested, and it is easy to imagine locals eagerly gathering at the warm forge to discuss events of the moment. To the blacksmith fell the task of putting new irons on the standard working footwear of the day – clogs. Whilst it was the cobbler-shoemaker who made the village footwear, it was the blacksmith who 'nebbed' or put studs in the clogs. Ernest Hill, the shoemaker in Redburn, boasted that his boots, shoes and clogs would last a lifetime, 'And, believe me, they looked as if they would too,' laughs Antoinette Wailes-Wilson, a former resident of nearby Henshaw village.

Florence Dunn, the shepherd's daughter of Kidlandlee, which is high in Coquetdale, on the south side of Cheviot, reports that Mr Forster of Harbottle made special boots for shepherds and strong shoes for their wives. She remembers her aunt wearing these sturdy shoes with a long, fringed, Otterburn tweed skirt.

The blacksmith was often also the farrier, just as the Hardings of Tow House (Tynedale) were. A farrier must be a cautious man who has empathy with horses. He approaches the animal from the near side and works on the near front foot first, moving round in an anti-clockwise direction to

Margaret Robson

Ernest Hill, the Redburn shoemaker.

clean the hoof and trim the horn with his paring knife and rasp. To complete the job, he tests the shoe for fit before fixing it with specially-shaped nails. This was never a job for the unskilled or clumsy. The nails have to be hammered into the horn of the hoof at exactly the right angle; if they touch the quick of the hoof, the horse will lash out and send the farrier flying.

Perhaps the greatest and most surprising change is that now, the few remaining farriers of the county, complete with their mobile forges, travel to the horses, rather than the horses coming to them.

Other venerable trades have also gone: there is little call for thatchers within the county – whether reed, straw or heather thatch is needed. Quarrymen are now few in number, as are the brickmakers. Milling tends to take place in industrial areas rather than in the country-

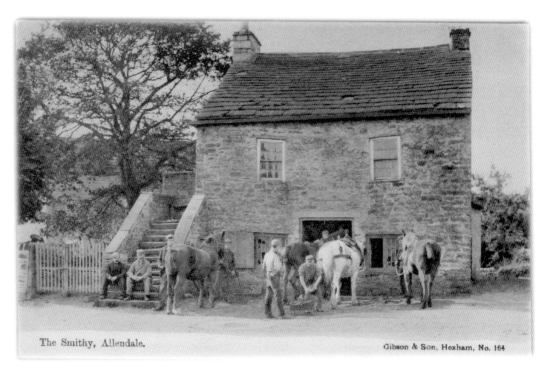

The Smithy, Allendale.   Gibson & Son, Hexham, No. 164

side. Farming has become an almost solitary occupation and there is also a huge decline in both mining and fishing.

Amongst the traditionally female trades, there has also been a great decline. For instance, hats and gloves would generally be worn out of doors. The 1851 census for Northumberland and Durham shows that there were 15 workers per 1000 involved in working with silk, straw, gloves, hats and stockings. By 1911 there are none. Olive Purves, Mrs Buglass, Minnie Craighead, Mildred Wright, as the affluent children of (respectively) a tobacconist, a butcher, an engineer and a bank manager, all report having had their clothes made for them by a dressmaker. Revealing a subtle distinction of social standing, Mrs Bolam recalls a Miss Barber calling at the house to do sewing, 'She was a very superior

woman who came for the day.'

Margaret Douglas's mother was a dressmaker in Amble and she was much sought after by the 'Herring Girls' who came each year.

Betsy Simpson of Ashington, a miner's daughter, was apprenticed to a dressmaker at the age of thirteen. 'I was dying to be a cook, but my mother insisted that I should serve my time as a dressmaker and paid a premium of two pounds. Mother couldn't sew herself and I often wondered whether she insisted on me being apprenticed to a dressmaker, so I could make her clothes for her.

I got paid one shilling a week, but the journeywoman I worked with had served her time at the Equitable Store and wasn't paid at all in the four years she was apprenticed. After a year I became what they called 'an improver' and then I earned four shillings a week. In those days, parents were keen their children should learn a trade, especially in the pit villages, anything rather than them go down the pit. My brother's friends were apprenticed to a baker, a butcher and a confectioner and Dad hoped that my brother would serve his time, but he insisted on going down the pit because the wages were better.'

She continues, 'In the workshop, we had to make up our own patterns for clothes and the patterns had to be right.' Dressmaking, however, was changing radically in the 1920s. There was a new system of measurement, the Haslam Sykes system, and it was much more scientific. 'I took extra lessons in the new technique which measured length, bust, waist and hips. Mother couldn't understand why I needed to go to extra lessons, but I knew things were changing and I needed to be up to date. We were still working without zips; fastening was done with lots of hooks and eyes, or buttons. Clothes had wads of padding; but the sort that mother and the older women wore was disappearing and everything was becoming lighter and more natural in shape.'

Milliners have disappeared, so too have most of the jobs in a field which once employed a considerable portion of the unmarried female population of the county: domestic service. What became available, especially for women, were jobs in shops. The spread of railway branch lines enabled goods to be delivered swiftly to country towns and villages and brought down food prices in the latter part of the 19th century. The Co-operative movement rapidly expand its stores throughout the county. Other retailers – for example, Liptons and Home & Colonial Stores – recognised the commercial advantage of expanding their customer range using horse-drawn mobile shops and delivery boys and girls on bicycles. Ethel Elliott, born near Red Row in the 1920s, travelled many miles of Northumberland on her bicycle before and after the Second World War, collecting and delivering orders for Brough's Groceries.

Sadly, those of us born in Northumberland later in the 20th century have witnessed the once unimaginable disappearance of coal-mining and ship-building. Our school geography assured us that Northumberland and Durham rested on huge deposits of coal, Lancashire was the 'Cotton King' and Yorkshire the home of the woollen trade. Nowadays, 'Coals to Newcastle' has little meaning as a saying; Lancashire's 'thread' which provided 'Britain's bread' became very frayed from the mid-part of the 20th century and the Yorkshire wool trade is much reduced. As for ship-building – a single yard remains on the Tyne, and the River Wear has none.

FARMERS AND SHEPHERDS SHOULD SEE OUR FAMOUS LAND BOOTS Made in horse hide (as illustrated) also in stout kip. PHONE: 1969. PRICE, 39/- (IDEAL FOR THE MOORS).

The pit

'No-one who hasn't worked down the pit
will ever understand the comradeship between miners.'

In 1938, at the age of fourteen, Jimmy Ditchburn, whose gardener father had died of peritonitis, started work down the pit at Ashington and was able to make some financial contribution to his widowed mother's household.

'I began by knocking on and knocking off, moved to flatting, cutting, filling and drawing and by then I earned 9s 6d a week. I had to hand over my pay packet to my mother and she gave me back 1s 6d pocket money, sixpence of which was to go to the pictures and the rest to do with as I liked. I loved dancing, so I'd go to the Princess Ballroom (in Ashington) or the Harmony.'

Jimmy, a keen cross country runner and fast sprinter, who had recently broken the record at the Five Counties Meet, had dreamed of professional athletics fame but a knee injury during his first week at the pit put an end to his running career.

'You'd come home after an eight-hour shift and then you'd clean all the mud off your boots wi' an old knife. Then you'd put them and your clothes to dry at the side of the fire while you scrubbed yourself in the tin tub in front of it. There were no pit baths in them days and there's many a miner wouldn't wash his back because they believed it weakened it. Then, when you'd had your meal, you'd shine your hats, boots and knee pads to keep the water out before you could sit down to rest.' (At Bardon Mill Colliery, throughout summer or winter, before the pit baths were erected, miners would walk along the railway track to reach the South Tyne at Redburn Pool where they would bathe off the coal dust permeating their pores before going home.)

In his forty years of working down the mines, Jimmy had many narrow escapes, 'I remember a bad one in 1957. I was drawing – that's taking out the day before's supports – and I

Ashington Colliery.

44

had but one plank to draw when "Howway and get your baits" was shouted, ['Bait' is the local term for the home-boxed lunch]. Now earlier that shift, I'd had a blazing row with a bloke at the next face. I can't even remember what it was about now, but it was a real blazer. Anyway, I drew away the last plank and a big stone fell out of the roof trapping me beneath it and choking me with the dust too. It was only a 2ft 3in seam, yet me marrers [workmates] lifted that rock away, but the devil knows how they did it and where they got the leverage from. I'd a broken collar bone and was bruised all over, and you know, the lad I'd had the row with was at the front of the rescuers! No-one who hasn't worked down the pit will ever understand the comradeship of miners. Perhaps only soldiers have that sort of close relationship with a marrer. You put your lives in each other's hands; rely on one another totally.'

Coalminers faced uncomfortable and dangerous conditions.

Jimmy is bitter about the way miners were treated, 'When you work down the pit, after four or five years the dust is in your lungs forever. Every miner suffers from pneumoconiosis to some degree. The work is hot, cramped, dirty and dangerous; not at all like standing in some production line in a light, clean factory. Yet in the 1970s, when the car workers were given a rise of £4 a week, we were given 6s 7d. Then in 1984, when the country had stores of natural gas and the government weren't afraid that British industry would grind to a halt without coal, they set the police on us for striking for our rights. I'd retired by then. I'd taken voluntary redundancy after forty years of working down there. I got a redundancy pension and compensation of £2,000. They promised me free coal too, but in the end I only got a single load per month – a quarter of what was promised – and I had also to pay rent for the colliery house I was in. What makes me really mad is that if I'd waited a couple of years, I'd have got £32,000 in voluntary redundancy.' Thinking over the conditions in which he worked for four decades, Jimmy believes that the best thing that happened in the mining industry was the war time Government's decision to send conscientious objectors down the mines – 'Bevan Boys', as they were known.

'Oh, aye, no doubt about it,' says Jimmy, 'posh lads, university educated, many of them from families with influence. They came in, saw how awful the job actually was and went away to tell everyone about it. And the "everyone" they knew were important people, or were going to be. You know, a lot of them lads ended up going into the army, rather than having to face going back down the pits.'

Betsy Simpson, the apprentice dressmaker mentioned in the previous chapter, recalls the miners' strike of 1926: 'The strike started in early May. Jack and me got married on May 23rd and were the first couple to get married in Lynemouth church. I'd no pay from my husband for eight months. How we managed, I don't know, but everyone else was hard up too. They opened a house in Lynemouth and you could go there and get vouchers for food, but Jack said he'd rather die than accept it. It was all right for us really, we went to live with my mother and we'd no children then. The men went back to work just before Christmas. He was working early shift on Christmas Day and we were waiting for him to come home after his shift. Mother had the Christmas dinner all ready to sit down to; instead, word came that he'd been badly hurt by a fall of stone on his back. They thought it'd broken his spine at first, but they sent him home from the hospital on New Year's Eve and he was back to work in a couple of months.

'It was always a worry, always in the back of your mind that they'd go off to work and you wouldn't see them alive again, or that you'd send out a fine, strong man and they'd have an accident which would cripple them for life.'

Barbara Coulthard, born in 1904, whose father was a miner and who married a miner herself, recalls the uncertainty of being a pitman's wife, 'My husband was a miner, but he so longed to be a farmer. We eventually got a colliery house with two rooms upstairs, a front parlour and a big kitchen. The wives would compete to have the cleanest washing and

Newcastle Daily Journal records getting back to work at Ashington pit after the 1926 strike.

the neatest step. My husband earned 30s a week in 1928, but if he got a cutter's job – the miners drew lots for the jobs – he could earn as much as £3. Mind you, if the buzzer went for work to finish that day, your heart sank because wages would be down. Good Fridays, Easter Monday and Whit Monday were always a problem because the pit was shut and you'd be short of wages that week; holidays weren't paid then.

'Mind you, even though we had no annual holiday, we'd take a picnic basket up to the hilly fields. We led a simple, contented life. We neither knew, nor wanted anything else. [Not entirely true, since Barbara had just said that her husband longed to be a farmer]. You'd been brought up to make do. You saw your parents mending, making, knitting, darning. The cats and dogs we had lived on the scraps. You bought a bottle of camphorated oil and rubbed that on the children's chests to ward off illness, or cure it. [But remember, miners also paid 6d per week to be on the doctor's panel of patients].

'I was six months pregnant with my second child when my husband was killed in the pit. My family were a great support and then the baby came and took up most of the sorrow. I got ten shillings a week compensation for myself, five shillings for my elder daughter and three shillings for the baby, when she was born. I moved in to my father's house and shared expenses. The payment stopped though the very

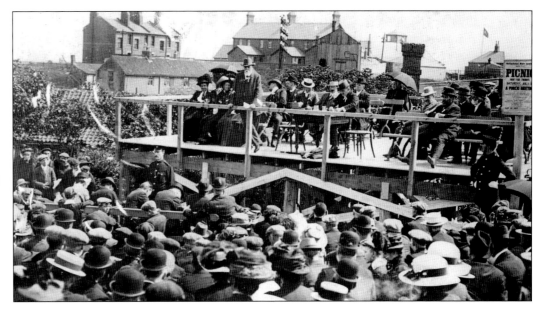

The Northumberland Miners' Picnic, Tynemouth, 1911.

day my younger daughter left school.'

Life in the mining communities was close and active. Most had thriving cricket and football clubs; there were bands, choirs, operatic societies and drama groups. Keen pigeon fanciers abounded, and for those who preferred four-legged beasts, there was the whippet racing. There was fierce competition in matters horticultural as miners grew glorious chrysanthemums, exuberant dahlias and giant leeks – the latter grown for the September Show and likely to bring big prizes. In Ashington, there was a thriving artists' group. As Mrs Coulthard says, no-one could afford holidays, so Sunday Schools, church groups and others organised trips to the coast and countryside. On summer days, whole streets of miners' wives would pack up sandwiches, ginger beer or pop and take the children to local beauty spots for picnics.

At Druridge Bay, the big event of the year was the Motor Cycle Race on the beach in August. In Ashington and Bedlington there were the Miners' Galas; indeed, throughout the county, miners proudly marched behind the colliery brass or silver band, colourful banners aloft.

Residents felt secure within their communities. Ned Thompson, born in 1918, says of his home village of East Chevington, 'Really! You could go away for a week and leave your door wide open and everything would be the same when you came back, except perhaps, somebody might have lit the fire for you. You knew everyone, and they knew you. If you did something wrong when you were a bairn and someone gave you a clip, you dursen't tell your Mam or Dad, or they'd give you another one. Then, we were a real community. We all helped each other.'

The former residents of East Chevington have good reason to feel some further resentment for the way they were treated. Not only did their livelihood vanish, but so did their village. East Chevington Drift mine was closed down in the 1960s; the National Coal Board claimed that the site was exhausted. The miners of East Chevington and the recently-closed Broomhill Pit – once the largest mine in the county – were without work. The economy of the district was ruined;

A Bedlington pigeon fancier, around 1910.

shops closed down, talented youngsters had no choice but to leave the area. The social life of the district, which had been strongly supported by the mineworkers, shrank to a pale shadow of what it had once been. In 1972 the villagers were relocated to Hadston in order that the site of their village – right on the edge of beautiful Druridge Bay – might be exploited for open cast mining. The residents of East Chevington were scattered throughout Hadston. Little effort was made to keep neighbours together. The community Ned Thompson remembers was no more.

Thirty-odd years on, the area is still struggling to recover from the blow. A small trading estate provides some employment and there are a couple of factories in nearby Amble. For most though, life is hard. There is little work for the menfolk and many of the women take on several part-time jobs to make ends meet. Amongst the elderly, retired miners there is still a sense of outrage. One told me, 'I never expected to have to give financial support to my adult children, but it happened. Now though, I'm giving help to my adult grandchildren too, because nothing has been done and the only way for them to get a job is to leave here. It's a sad thing when the only way to get on is to leave your family behind.'

Hirings

*'The farmers would view them up and down
as if they were horses.'*

In 1901, according to the Office for National Statistics (ONS), 13 per cent of the total labour force was employed in agriculture, forestry and fishing. By 2000, this was down to 2 per cent.

In Northumberland, as already mentioned, farmworkers were known as 'hinds' and were hired from year to year, their contracts running from 12 May. During March, Hiring Fairs were held in the main market towns throughout the county (Alnwick, Hexham, Morpeth, Wooler). The Hirings for shepherds, however, took place in January, since March was the beginning of the lambing season. Domestic workers were hired on a six-monthly basis and the fairs for these were in May and November. Moving, also known as 'Flitting Day', or 'The Flit', was traditionally 12 May.

The Hiring Fairs were a great occasion for meeting old friends and were also extremely popular with children. Stalls were set out in the market place and carefully-hoarded half-pennies allowed children to buy licquorice, lollipops, toffee or biscuits. Holidays were so very rare that any festive occasion was welcomed.

May Douglas recalls, 'My father went to the Hirings at Alnwick. We moved around a lot, but kept coming back to Bamburgh which I loved.' Not surprising, when Bamburgh has a glorious coastline, lovely countryside and splendid castle.

May remembers that her father would be given a shilling

Alnwick Market Place around 1900.

once he had agreed pay and conditions with the farmer (others report anything up to 2s 6d). This payment was known as 'the arles' and when accepted meant that the deal was contractually binding on both parties.

In the early 19th century, a hind's conditions of service included a free cottage, coals, grazing hay or straw for one cow, corn for bread, and potatoes. By the end of the century, although his wages had risen to around 17s 6d per week, his entitlements had shrunk to a free cottage, coals and potatoes.

Flora Thompson's splendidly evocative account of an Oxfordshire village in the 1870s, *Lark Rise to Candleford*, describes a life of great poverty amongst the farm workers; however, the earnings of agricultural labourers in both Northumberland and Durham were considerably better than their contemporaries in southern counties throughout the 19th and early 20th centuries. Board of Agriculture reports show that this advantage was maintained until the First World War.

May Douglas comments, 'Sometimes a man would stay in the same place for years and years and then he'd want a change. Or sometimes the farmers' sons would become old enough to work and the hind wouldn't be needed any more. If a farmer wanted a man to stay, he had to talk to him about it before the Hirings, or the man would assume he wasn't

Morpeth Market Place around 1890.

needed any more.'

May's observation underlines the uncertainties of a system which relied on annual hiring of labour. It did, however, work both ways: a farmer was obliged to offer decent conditions of work if he wished to retain good labourers; but on the other hand he could lose a troublesome hind without problems. A hind could leave for whatever reason he chose; he was a free man at the end of each annual contract. The Hiring system itself may well reflect the fact that so few

Northumbrians in feudal times were tied men.

The uncertainty of the whole Hirings business is what Evelyn Telfer, born in 1914 at Blagdon, also a shepherd's daughter, recalls: 'The family belongings were piled high on the horse and cart, but you never knew what you were going to. Often, the houses were quite poor and inadequate. I remember we were once given a cottage with a dirt floor in the kitchen, which was really just a wooden shack attached to the back of the house. There was no range, so mother had to cook on the open fire. The roof leaked too; the farmer kept promising to mend it, but he was too mean to do so. We all hated it and we moved on sharpish at the end of the year.'

Elizabeth Ann Luck recounts her family's first experience of using a motorised truck for 'The 'Flit'. 'Dad was so proud that he'd got Joe Pearson to move us in his new motor vehicle. Joe was a carrier with a business in Consett and another in Newcastle and was always up to date. Mother and my younger sister took the pony and trap whilst Dad and me went with the furniture. Well, the motor wouldn't pull up the bank at Ebchester we were so loaded, so

we had to go right round by Shotley Fields to get to Whittonstall. Mother had been there for hours by the time we arrived and she was beginning to get really anxious. The farmer, Mr Graham, was concerned too, but I think that he thought Dad might have changed his mind and wasn't coming. I was just very, very hungry.'

Isabella Keen, one of ten children of a hind, recollects that on one 'Flit' they made, the family had to make up a bed in a tiny attic room which had no window. You may remember from Chapter 1 that she and her five sisters already slept three to a bed, and two double beds were squashed into one room.

At the beginning of the 20th century, according to a

The new accommodation might be good, or very poor.

Board of Agriculture report, around five million women worked, making up a total of 29 per cent of the total work force (In 1961 the figure was $37^1/_2$ per cent; by the year 2000, around 53 per cent of women – by now calculated as those over the age of sixteen – worked).

In Northumberland, in the early part of the 20th century, many of these women worked in agriculture, a situation which was certainly not typical of the rest of the country. Figures show that in 1871, women in the county accounted for 22 per cent of the agricultural labour force, whilst the average for England and Wales was less than $3^1/_2$ per cent. These figures changed little before the First World War.

May Douglas remarks: 'My aunt was a bondager [a female field-worker, provided by the hind and paid by the day by him] and she used to say that they'd stand on the cobbles at Alnwick and the farmers would come and view them up and down as though they were horses.'

The work was hard, heavy and poorly-paid, compared with men's work; although it must be said that when, in 1918, the Agricultural Wages Board fixed a standard legal minimum for females, parts of Northumberland, along with Cumberland, Westmoreland and Yorkshire were excepted because women's wages were already higher than the minimum. For instance, in the Glendale Union, Northumberland, women were paid at the rate of 1s 4d to 1s 6d per day, whereas in parts of Norfolk they earned a mere 1s per day. The problem of the inequality

Haymakers, Coxlodge, 1902. Their bonnets are home-sewn white cambric (fine linen or cotton). The deep side flaps and neck flaps protected the face from the sun. All women wore headgear out of doors; bare heads were considered improper. Poor women, without hats or bonnets would pull their shawls over their heads to cover them. Even indoors many of the older women would wear lace or cotton caps until the early 20th century. Shawls were everyday outerwear, always woollen, either home-knitted or of finely-woven woollen cloth. In Northumberland the shawl was often a small black and white check known as Northumbrian Tartan or Shepherd's Plaid. For women, jackets and coats were strictly Sunday-best.

of women's wages is far from new, as one can see from this 19th century letter of complaint written by a group of bondagers to Farmer George Pickering of Stone Hall,

Henshaw. The letter is amongst Ruth Forster's papers, and I am grateful for her permission to reproduce it.

George Pickering was a farmer at Stone Hall, Henshaw in the mid-19th century. No date, names, nor signatures are on the paper. It looks as if someone had marked the mistakes with a pencil.

Isabella Keen eventually left home at fifteen to become a farmworker herself. 'It was haymaking time when I started. The hay was cut with a reaper and then there was a horse and bogey to load the hay, which was then stacked into big stack pikes. There were lots of helpers for haymaking and

the harvest. Many of the married women would come along to earn a few shillings, they'd leave their small babies and small children in the charge of their mothers or young daughters. Young lads would often find some employment in busy times of the year.'

Below are two entries in the Henshaw School log, a year after compulsory schooling was introduced:

May 9th, 1873: A number of children have left this week … leaving neighbourhood … left to be hired.

May 23rd, 1873: Made enquiries concerning absentees … principally girls … in consequence of their mothers being employed about the farms at the present time, they require the girls at home to attend to household duties.

Similar entries appear each year for the next fifty years

Milkmaids at a Northumberland farm c.1900.

during haymaking and harvest times.

Mr Robinson, who was born in Bedlington in 1918, and whose father was a miner, was sent to spend all of his summer holiday from school in Rothbury with an aunt; eventually his family moved to the village. His best friend was an orphan named Joe Beswick, and working with Joe put Mr Robinson off farming for life.

'The supervisor came and asked my aunt whether she would take him in. His own aunt didn't want to take him in, so he'd been put in a home. He hadn't done anything wrong, but people were suspicious of lads from those places. [Not only orphans, but boys or girls judged to be in need of 'reformatory care', were frequently placed in orphanages]. Anyway, he came to live with my aunt. Joe had been taught farming and he'd go round all the farms looking for work. At that time, I really liked the notion of farming. Anyway, one summer day Joe came and said that there was a week's work for both of us at a farm, if I wanted to go with him. I went along and the farmer had us chopping down thistles in the field opposite the Almshouses – the field is part of the golf course now. It was hot, hard work and we worked from dawn to dusk, but we'd been promised a good wage at the end of it – five shillings each for the week. When we'd cleared the thistles, he set us to going round another field with the seed fiddle. We

Fields around the almshouses at Rothbury, where Mr Robinson was put off farming for life.

finished the whole job at sundown on the Saturday and went to collect our pay, and you know what? The farmer diddled us! He handed us 2s 6d each and said that was the agreed price. It quite put me off farm work.'

A number of the women contributors entered domestic service, many of them on farms. Farm work was considered to be at the very bottom of the hierarchy of domestic service: a judgement more to do with snobbery than with actual conditions of service, which were often better than those in a private household. It was customary for the hinds to take their breakfast at the farmhouse, so fires had to be lit early for fresh bread to be baked. The farmer and his labourers all sat down to bacon, sausages, eggs and fried bread – all home-produced – at the kitchen table each morning after the milking or other early morning tasks were completed. After their own breakfast, the dishes were washed and the women would be involved in egg collection, butter-making, cheese-making, baking, domestic cleaning and laundry. On top of this would be the seasonal tasks of bottling and preserving fruit and vegetables, curing ham and bacon, making sausages and black (or white) puddings, or salting beef.

Florence Dunn, born at Kidlandlee and wife of shepherd Tom Dunn, devised a recipe for bottling chicken in aspic; this proved so popular with the Duke of Northumberland's shooting party guests that they carried away her entire stock (unpaid) as samples for their own cooks. Florence regarded this as a compliment, rather than a thoughtless liberty!

Farms were independent units, able to provision themselves and providing jobs for a small community around them. Until the advent of tractors – which occurred for some farms during the 1930's, but for most after World War Two – a farmer would be surrounded by employees and their families. However, with the advent of the Fordson tractor – a ubiquitous mechanical horse – the whole nature of farming changed; consequently, nowadays, farms employ few, if any, workers outside of the immediate family. The tied cottages which would once have housed the workers have been converted into holiday homes or sold off to city commuters.

Mr Price, born at Newton by the Sea, recalled how his father bought a farm near Berwick in 1927 and within a year was almost bankrupt because food prices dropped so low. (In 1932, grain prices were at their lowest for 150 years). Had it not been for an uncle, they would have gone under. Only when World War Two broke out did prices rise. For him, though, the greatest change in farming is to see the ubiquitous planting of wheat and rape on land which used to grow

The Newcastle Journal for 30 November 1931 advertises plenty of agricultural work for women.

barley, oats, turnips and potatoes.

A greater change in the countryside, perhaps, is in social attitudes. In the early part of the 20th century there was huge deference and respect for the local landowner and his wife who provided much employment in the district with his patronage. The vicar, doctor, schoolteacher and large-holding farmers also commanded deference and would expect to be patrons of local ventures, for example, the establishment of a Reading Room in a village, a popular addition to village facilities. Whilst many of the contributors claim that contentment with one's lot and knowing one's place were key factors in their own upbringing, all who became parents admit to having had greater ambitions for their own children.

After World War One, changes in social attitudes accelerated and became more apparent, particularly among labouring men. Not only did soldiers return from the trenches with a conviction that they could do as well, if not better, than the 'officer class', but their wives and sweethearts too had found themselves doing war work alongside county 'toffs', and often doing it more ably than their so-called 'betters'.

A million and a half men had died in the trenches. At home, their families had suffered great privations and very little had been done to relieve the wives of serving soldiers, or their widows and children, a number of whom struggled on the edge of starvation without a man's (larger) income to support them. Social unrest was growing; deference was slowly dissipating; it seemed that the working classes were no longer content with their lot.

Although now often scoffed at, mistakenly, as the 'Jam and Jerusalem brigade', the Women's Institute was a seminal organisation of that time, particularly with regard to rural women. An idea imported from the Dominion of Canada, it was to bring together women of all classes, without distinction. The Northumberland Federation of Women's Institutes was formed in 1918 with the aim of ensuring that women should be informed and educated in matters concerning their community. Meetings were often held on nights of the full moon because roads were uneven and unlit. Despite a national constitution which determined that all women should be eligible for membership regardless of religion, class or marital status (an entirely new concept, directly attributable to the Women's Suffrage movement) in the earliest days of the organisation, old habits died hard and the 'lady at the Big House' expected to be invited to become president of her local branch, and often was. Egalitarian efforts were being made, however, and a request from the National Federation in 1922 asks branches to recommend 'the names of women of the cottage-type for co-option to the National Executive'. This suggests, despite the patronising language, that poorer women were regarded as worthy committee members.

May Telfer sums up the wide-reaching social changes and her own deference rather neatly, 'Who'd have thought that I'd have a son who would lunch with the Duke of Westminster and then fly home to have supper with the shepherds at their Annual Meet up at Harbottle. He's also lunched with the Prince of Wales, and the Princess Royal too. [Mrs Telfer's son is a land-agent]. In my young days, remembering that I am the daughter of a decent, but ordinary farmer, who would ever have forecast that one day my own son would meet and lunch with royalty.'

Maureen Brook

Women's Institute, Bothal, late 1940s.

Fisherfolk of Newbiggin

'Fisherlife was very hard. The men took the risks, there were many drownings.'

Chris Blandford was raised in Newbiggin by the Sea. His mother was one of the fisherfolk and, most unusually, she was married to a miner. Chris gives a lively account of life in Newbiggin in the early part of the 20th century.

'We lived in a stone cottage on Main Street. There were six cottages on one side of the street and five on the other. An outside tap was provided for each row and, in winter, we had to pack around the tap with straw and set it alight to unfreeze it. There was a row of outside toilets too. They had really thin partitions between them and you could hear everything that was said. People used to converse with their neighbours while sitting on the netty (dialect for lavatory; said to come from the Victorian term, 'necessary'). Of course then there was no such luxury as toilet paper. We cut up newspaper into squares and hung it from string.

'Inside the house, there were two large rooms up and two down. My sister shared a bed with Granny, who lived with us, and my parents had the other bedroom. My brother and me slept in a desk bed in the kitchen.

'My parents were given the chance of a council house in Ashington, but Granny didn't want to leave the fisherfolk, so they gave the keys back to the council and moved into an old house. Really, the problem was that the fisherfolk deeply dis-

Newbiggin fisherwomen around 1900.

approved of the miners and their ways. Miners drank and gambled, the fisherfolk – strong Methodists – were dead against drink and gambling. Every Saturday night, my father would wash and dress himself – and he was a natty dresser – to go out to the Club. Every Saturday night, Mother would knock off his cap when he'd got it just so. He'd call her his "drunken minny" which would make her wild as she was strictly teetotal. She'd get her own back when he came home roaring drunk and she'd yell insults at him. I must say though, in all the years, he never once struck my mother, however drunk he was.

'Fisher life was very hard. The men took the risks and there were many drownings. The women's job was to untangle the line, clean it up and then bait it again. They had to skairn [open] the mussels they picked from the rocks earlier that day and set seven to eight hundred of them on the hooks. Then they furled the line just so, so the line would run out itself from the boat. Many a women lost fingers through getting them caught on the hooks: the finger would go septic and would have to come off before the septicaemia spread. The line itself was like three or four hundred yards of twine – a bit like an extra-long washing line – and then there was the cord with the hook snood [in true Northumbrian fashion, Chris pronounces this as 'heuksnud']. My mother's lines would come back with a fish on every hook. Mostly they caught cod, whiting and haddock. The men had gutting hooks for the big fish and I've seen huge skates and ling hanging from these.

'Of course, poor fishermen got poor catches. A good fisherman looked after his gear. I remember a bloke called White-headed Neddie; he was called that because he was an albino with white hair and red eyes. Now Ned was not a good fishermen, he used gear that others would throw away because the cord was rotten. My Uncle Christopher would put away money for new gear, but Ned was feckless like that. Ned's mother and father were called Sparra and Old Mal. When I was very little, they had this big cat which frightened me. Anyway, as I got older, they became bedridden. White-headed Ned was at sea and Granny got worried because she hadn't seen or heard them for days, so she sent me in to see if they were alright. Well, Sparra and Old Mal were in bed in a sorry state. They wanted a drink of tea, but all I could find in the cupboards was some dried-up lemon peel. I went back and told Granny. She promptly handed me sixpence and said to go get some fish and chips for them. Eh, you'd think I'd given them £1000 from the way they went on. Yes, Granny kept an eye out for them. When the old folks died, Ned had the decency to pay back some of the money she'd lent them over the years from the insurance money. He gave her £15, which was a lot in them days, but it was probably just a drop in the ocean to what she'd given.

'There were mainly four families – the Armstrongs, the Robinsons, the Browns and the Dawsons. Many of them had the same name, so all the fisherfolks were given identifying nicknames. There was Bella Flathat – she always wore a cap; Harry Frenchy – he wasn't a full shilling and babbled nonsense; Ned the Whaler – he and his two sons were drowned when they were salmon fishing and they were dragged down. The boat was recovered and is still going to sea yet. There was Billy the Whaler and Ned the Whaler, his brother. I think that Billy got his name because a whale got washed ashore and Billy climbed into its jaws and had his photo taken. Mop used to do all the fetching and carrying and he always wore a fur hat; Watson's Willie was coxswain of the lifeboat; Dick

Baiting the lines at Newbiggin around 1900.

the Miller's horses pulled the lifeboat up and down the beach when it was needed. I recall the wrecking of a Norwegian boat called the *Arctic Skua*, mainly because there was a woman on board, as well as the five crew, and our fishermen were horrified. They never had women on board a boat – it was bad luck! They got them all off before she was swamped. They were all given medals, but they'd never talk about it.

'Back to the characters: let's see, there was Geordie Raff, who was really George Taylor, Jackie the Peg – and where he got that name from, I don't know, 'cos he didn't have a wooden leg. My cousin Kit was known as Hunter Kit and my uncle as Geordie Kit. There was Darkie Tom, he was a Dawson, dark-haired and dark-skinned like the other Dawsons. His sister was known as Black Hannah. My Uncle William was known as Pete's Wull and his son was Bob's Wul, why I don't know. Pin was the captain of the lifeboat. Then there was Hawkie's Belle who

The Newbiggin lifeboat ready for launching.

used to clean the school. She'd bait her hooks and then do her cleaning, so sometimes it would be two in the morning when she was at the school. One night she shovelled up this heap of what she thought was coal and brought a bucket of it home, nearly smoking out the whole terrace. It wasn't coal at all, it was black pitch for mending the roads.

'When the boats came in – they had sails and oars in those days – everyone helped pull them ashore. The men would hang onto the back to keep the boat up, so as the wheels could be put underneath to roll them up the beach. The women would be up to their waists in water. Darkie Tom's mother once asked him to keep an eye on the bread she was baking while she went to help with the boats. "When you can smell it, take it out, Tom". Well, when she came back, the bread was still in the oven and burnt to a crisp. She shouted at him, but he replied, "Eh, woman, you locked the oven door and I didn't know how to get it open." Then, a man had no idea of anything domestic. Tom didn't even know how to lift the handle of an oven.

'When the women weren't collecting mussels or baiting lines, they were knitting the ganseys [jerseys] for the men. Each family had its own individual cable pattern. Bodies have been identified by the pattern on the ganseys they wore.

Newbiggin girls pose for the camera c.1900. The centre girl, who is knitting a gansey, wears a traditional skirt which might be between calf- and ankle-length. The tucks around the lower part (the number of tucks being personal preference) helped to keep the legs warm whilst baiting hooks out of doors and also prevented the skirts from bunching uncomfortably while walking. A number of petticoats would be worn underneath in winter but reduced to one or two in summer. The girls on either side are in their 'best dresses'. These were usually a brightly coloured brocade fabric – scarlet, emerald, magenta and sapphire blue were popular. These shades were relatively new and made possible with the analine dyes of the late 19th century.

'It was a hard life for women. No fisherman would have dreamt of bringing in a wife from outside; she wouldn't have been able to cope with the work. My Granny had kept house for my Uncle Willie until her fingers were crippled with arthritis. Then she told him he'd have to find himself a wife. Well, Uncle Willie was in his late thirties and had missed the boat, so to speak; all the pretty lasses of his own age had long gone. The only available female was Lang Taylor. Aunt Taylor was another Dawson, with the dark skin and dark eyes, and she was tall. Some called her The Big Apache. Uncle Willie asked her to marry him and she said she would. And do you know, it was a very happy match. She was an expert at everything you'd expect of a fisherman's wife, so Uncle Willie felt he'd made a good choice, even though there hadn't been much choice in it. Every Sunday night, they would come up to Aunt Bella's to hand over ten shillings for Granny. I'm sure that half the time they had to take that money out of the savings for the new gear, but they felt duty-bound to pay for their share of Granny's keep when she was living with us, more especially because my dad was a miner. They couldn't hand over the money to Granny herself because she wouldn't speak to Uncle Willie after the fight.

'The fight? Well, you see, there was always great rivalry between the Armstrongs and the Dawsons about who caught the most fish. It only wanted a small spark to set off a blazing row. Now Jackie Arkle was married to my cousin, Sarah Jane Armstrong and one night Jackie and his brother, Tommy Arkle, came in drunk. Bella, Tommy's wife, who was a Dawson, blamed Jackie. Sarah Jane's brother, Bobby Armstrong, and Jackie then began fighting about it on the Sunday morning. A proper, coats-off fight, mind you. At that point, all the Armstrongs, and I mean all of them, set about

The pit at Newbiggin, 1931.

62

the Dawsons to teach them a lesson – the men were punching at each other, the women were scratching at eyes and tearing out clumps of hair, even the dogs joined in and were snapping and biting at one another. What a carry on it was!

'Uncle Willie, being newly-married to a Dawson, felt he'd better keep well out of it, so he did. However, Granny heard that he'd ducked the fight and, from then on, she wouldn't speak to him because he hadn't upheld the honour of the Armstrongs.

'During the summer, there'd be lots of people. The place would be full of chara-bancs. There were lots of day-trippers, but others took a house for a few weeks. I'd take a ball of string to the rocks and some loose pieces [fish bits] and I'd fish for mackerel or herring, which I'd sell to them for their meals. I made many a copper during the summer holidays, sometimes as much as five or six shillings a week, which was very good pocket money for a kid. I'd have a great time on Lifeboat Day or when the carnivals came.

'When I left school, I could have joined the fisherfolk, but to be honest, I was scared of the sea and had never learned to swim, so I became a miner like my father. Granny would have been shocked to see me drinking the beer and enjoying whippet racing with the best of them. My best whippet was a little bitch called 'Bonny Heather', she won loads of money for me. Then the war came along and I joined the Royal Marine Commandoes. Afterwards, I returned to the pits and was there until I retired.

Trippers at Newbiggin, 1936.

'Over the years I've watched the beach at Newbiggin change greatly. Once it had smooth, silvery sands and lots of visitors. Now though, coal washings have polluted it and there are very few visitors. Nature, too, seems determined to change Newbiggin. St Bartholomew's Church, which has stood at Newbiggin Point for 700 years, is now perilously close to the sea and I wonder how much longer we'll see it standing there? The fishing too has just about gone, along with the cod which used to be so common. It feels strange to have been so much part of a bygone way of life'.

Trawlermen

'The trawler rocked and rolled in the swell.
The mast and rigging were thick with ice and snow.'

Bob Duff vividly recalls a River Tyne full of shipping and his life as a trawlerman: 'From the Fish Quay and the docks at Howdon, past Wallsend and Hebburn, right up to the Newcastle Quayside, the boats would be three and four abreast, shipping was so prolific. There were coal staithes all up the river and the collier brigs would be passing up and down as soon as the tide allowed. You could take a collier down to London if you wanted a cheap way of travelling. Of course, there was no Tyne Bridge [not until 1928] then and the river was extremely dirty. It's a lot cleaner now; I understand they even catch salmon in it again.

'I lived in a terraced house on Tynemouth Road, North Shields. We were very comfortable. We had a front room – most people only used them for weddings and funerals – a back living room where we had the piano, and then you went along a passage to the kitchen where there was the big, black range which mother polished endlessly, that and the brass fire-irons. Upstairs, there were three bedrooms and a bathroom with hot water heated from the kitchen range. I was the fourth in a family of six children – four boys and two girls. We used to love going down to the Fish Quay. If the boats were coming in, they'd give you a bit of fish to take home for your tea.

'We all went to Christ Church school and all we lads were in the church choir.

'My father was a skipper on a trawler, so during the school holidays, he'd take us out to sea on pleasure trips, teaching us about fishing. Then, when we got to about thirteen, he'd send us down to Irvine's stores where they made

Christ Church, North Shields, c.1935.

64

the nets and we were given spools and taught about all the meshes and how to repair them. As a trawlerman it was essential to know how to repair nets which were torn on wreckage or rocks.

'At fourteen, I left school and went to join my father on the trawler. Even though you were young, you mixed in with the rest of the crew and were expected to pull your weight. Each boat had a crew of ten: the skipper, the mate, third hand, three deckies, the cook, the fireman, two lads. We earned 8s 6d per day, less two shillings a day for your food. Each trip to sea lasted eight to ten days.

'Summertime was best, usually the weather was quite mild then, but we went out the whole year round. It was

The Tyne at North Shields around 1890. Beyond the paddle steamers is the Fish Quay and rows of herring boats with their black sails. The High Lights, centre, and the Low Lights, right, guided ships through the perilous entrance to the river.

the skipper's decision as to where we would fish – usually, years of experience told him where would be best. For instance, if we wanted flatfish like plaice, halibut, lemon sole (my own personal favourite) which live on small eels on sandbanks, the skipper would check the charts for sandbanks and we'd run, say, 70 or 80 miles from the Tyne. When we arrived at a likely spot, down would go a lead weight with a hollow

in the bottom. This hollow would have been filled with tallow, so if there was sand on it when it came up, then we were above a sandbank and in a likely spot for the catch we were after. Over would go what's called the "Dan", which is a buoy with an anchor on the bottom of it, and we'd fish round that.

'Now if we were after cod or ling, we'd have to make for

rocky ground – mainly around Iceland. So it was out of the Tyne, head north to Peterhead, Pentland Firth, Orkneys, Shetlands, Faroe and Iceland. There'd be lots of damage to the nets, but in those days, the fishing was good round Iceland. Mind you, by the time I retired in 1982, the North Sea was already becoming depleted and ships were having to go further afield for decent catches.

'Fishing off Iceland in winter was hard. The boats got iced up; the rigging down to the sides of the ships got thick with snow and, instead of being steady, the trawler would roll and rock in the swell. You'd have to keep hitting the wire rigging, "chipping" we called it, to get rid of the weight of ice to stop it dragging us over; then the decks would have to be shovelled clear of snow and ice. Meanwhile, you're dragging the nets behind, picking up the catch. When the net was full, you'd bring it alongside, put a rope around the mast and heave it up. The third hand would then get underneath the net and loosen the rope we called the "cod end" which held in the catch. Once that rope was pulled away, the catch would come tumbling down onto the deck. Then we'd tie the rope in again and toss the net overboard to trawl behind us again. At that point, we'd begin preparing the catch for the fish room, which was below deck. You took a very sharp knife and took out the liver and innards of each fish, you threw the fish into a basket and the offal overboard. While you were doing that, the boat was still pitching and rolling, and you mind that you were holding a very sharp knife. Yes, many a cut, or a bit of finger was lost at that stage. Once the basket was full, you threw it down the hatch to the fish room where it was packed in chopped ice and put on a shelf. You did that repeatedly until the shelves of the fish room were full, then you came home.

'After the First World War, sometimes you'd catch a more deadly cargo – mines! The sort with horns sticking out of the sides, which, if they touched the sides of the boat, would detonate.

'Once, when we were fishing off the Norwegian coast, a mine dropped out of the net amongst the catch. Now we'd only just got there, but if you picked up a mine, "a dangerous cargo", as it was known, you were supposed to run for home, inform the coastguard, who'd ring the army or navy to come and detonate it safely. Of course, that meant losing out on that trip's profit, so we were reluctant to turn back. Anyway, we spliced some ropes round the mine and then tied them to the mast. The mine swung above us as the trawler rolled and we watched it swinging. The minute we got a really good roll, we all yelled 'Leggo!' The mate cut the ropes, the mine dropped away into the sea and the helmsman swung us away from it. Mind you, I think we were all a bit nervous that we'd come across it again.

'The worst trip I ever made was one in which when we were off the Shetlands, we lost our rudder in a gale and were being forced inshore towards the rocks. We were getting desperate, because no rudder means no steering. Anyway, the skipper called us together and said that he was going to try and use the trawlboards – the boards which keep the nets open whilst they're underwater – as a jury-rudder. The trawlboards are fitted with holes, called shekels, through which you run wires. The skipper fitted a board under the back of the trawler and brought us back into the Tyne. It was a terrific feat of seamanship.

'I retired when I was 72, and by then I'd reached Mate. During the Second World War, I did have a few years out, mind you.

'I got married in 1938 and decided I'd had enough of the sea, so I left it and went off to Rutherford College in Newcastle to learn to be an electrician. When I got the exams, I joined Rediffusion, which was, I suppose, cable wireless, like they have cable television nowadays; I put in feeder leads to all the houses. Anyway, then the war came along and suddenly there wasn't enough copper wire to use for cable, so they laid a few of us off. I decided that I fancied being in the Air Force, so I went along with some of the others to the Recruiting Office in Newcastle, where they said, "An electrician? Just the chappies we need."

We went for training and I think we all hoped we'd get posted south; really I hoped for some tropical island, to get a chance to

The fishing boat Nellie Wilson with her crew. This photograph was taken at Berwick upon Tweed.

see somewhere exotic in the world. Now then, you'll never guess where they sent me? Would you believe it, I was seconded to the American Airforce in – of all places – Iceland! I spent three very quiet years there before they brought me back to England, posted me to Thorney Island in Hampshire to work on the big transporter planes, before I was finally discharged. After that, I went back to the trawlers – and Iceland – again.'

The herring girls

'They adored bright brocades in jewel-like colours.'

The arrival of the herring shoals meant a busy time for fishing communities on the coast of Northumberland. May Telfer recalls how the teams of 'Herring girls' would be put up in lofts in North Sunderland and would gut the catches as they were brought in. The herring girls moved down the east coast of Britain from the north of Scotland to Great Yarmouth from late April until early October and their arrival brought other business for local people, not least of all the coopers whose barrels were needed for the salted herring. There were other less obvious beneficiaries, for example, Margaret Douglas's mother, who was a skilled dressmaker:

'Each year, the women would arrive in Seahouses in late June or early July. They got paid when the season was over and every year part of their earnings would go to buying a bolt of cloth for a new dress. They would then take the bolt home to Scotland with them and store it in the recessed cupboard next to the fire to keep it dry. They had peat fires in their cottages, so the cloth always had this delicious, peaty smell to it. The following year, they'd bring last year's cloth along with them to take to their favourite dressmaker to have their dress made. The cloth was always brocade and they adored bright, jewel-like colours. My

North Sunderland, around 1910.

mother was one of their favourites and she'd have less than a fortnight to make up to 14 dresses – made entirely to measure. They weren't simple frocks. No, they'd all have tiny pleats and tucks, leg-o-mutton sleeves and be padded and boned according to the latest fashion. They were party gowns and I think the women wore them to the ceilidhs and weddings.

'Mother was from Seahouses. She and Father got married in the month of June. And they went to live in Amble. A week after the wedding, Grandpa Tait wrote to Mother from Seahouses saying, "Annie, you've got to come home! The herring girls are sitting on the doorstep crying because you're not here to make their dresses." So mother took her tape measure and went back to Seahouses overnight. She took all the measurements, collected the bolts of cloth, came home and within the fortnight had made all the dresses and delivered them back to the girls.

'Of course, nothing was ever wasted in those days, so when my twin sister and I came along, mother taught us to sew using those scraps of material and our house was peppered with jewel-bright cushions. I still have one and it still smells faintly of peat smoke.'

[Miss Douglas hands me a bright cushion, which does indeed have the faintly sweet, smoky odour of peat clinging to it].

'Every year we'd go up to Seahouses and stay with Grandfather and Grandmother Tait. Mother would make the dresses and we'd go down to the Herring Sheds and peep in and all the girls would start twittering, "Look! There's Annie Tait's twinnies, wave to them!" And they'd all be waving to us. My sister Isabelle and I loved it.' (The twins are pictured on page 30.)

Margaret Atiken

Margaret Douglas wearing a suit made by her dressmaker mother.

Following the shoals right down the east coast from spring to autumn. The 'Herring Girls' worked in crews of three – two gutters and a packer. Most of them lived in dormitories above the herring sheds, such as the lofts in Seahouses which May Telfer recalls. Once the catch was in the 'Girls' worked long shifts, often from 6 a.m. until the early hours of the following morning. A good team could earn up to ten shillings a day (very good pay then), although their earnings were not paid until the end of the season. The curers paid them eight shillings a week for their lodgings and the food they bought for themselves (deducted eventually from the total sum earned). The cost of the lodgings

Fisher girls from Scotland at Seahouses around 1900.

was usually about three or four shillings a week and most landladies would offer to cook the food the women bought. The work was not only hard but hazardous, for the gutting knife had to be extremely sharp. To protect themselves, the women wrapped their fingers in strips of cloth made out of densely-woven flour sacks; the threads from the sacks were used to tie on the strips. All the same, there were accidents, and cuts were made agonisingly painful because of the brine with which the women worked.

Once sorted into sizes and gutted, the fish was soaked in brine and packed tightly into the 4ft high barrels. Usually the packer had to climb into the barrel to pack the first layer.

The layers were laid in a rosette pattern (head in, tail out, first layer; tail in, head out, second layer, etc.). A thick coating of salt was then laid over the layers and tamped down to prevent the layers from touching. When full, the barrels were left standing for ten days until the salt and the juices had mingled, then the remaining juice (blood pickle) would be drained off. The barrels were then re-packed up to the top, since the fish would have shrunk during the process, before being sealed and laid on their sides. The blood pickle was poured back into a hole in the lid of the barrel. The hole was then bunged. There would be roughly 900-1200 fish per barrel.

Kippering was a different process and is said to have been accidentally discovered in Seahouses in 1843 by John Woodger, when some split herring were left in a shed where a fire had continued burning all night. The catch was at first considered 'ruined', until someone tasted it and the kipper was born!

Further down the coast in North Shields, the herring catch was brought straight to the fish sheds where local women gutted them and prepared them for kippering. Margaret Compson, born in 1918 at North Shields, longed to work in the fish smokery, but her mother, who had experience of the work, refused to allow it. All the same, during lunch breaks at school, Margaret loved going down to the Fish House in Reid Street to watch the women work. She learned that a fish containing 'slim' (roe) was more valuable, for a good price was paid for herring roes. She'd then watch the women taking the fish to the 'trow' to drain before being placed in the 'pickle' (salt dye) and then passed to another trough, and finally hung on tenterhooks which were placed in the smokehouse. As a young girl, the men had allowed her to climb the 'lumbs' in the smokehouse and get covered in dye. She loved it all, but her mother could not be persuaded that it was the life for her daughter.

'In them days you did what your parents told you to do. You had no choice,' Margaret says ruefully. For two years she worked reluctantly for a baker, delivering bread and teacakes to old people who couldn't get out to do shopping, 'I'd take their loaves. I'd walk miles for twopence a loaf and twopence for four teacakes. I used more shoe leather than I earned in pay.'

When she reached sixteen, she again approached her mother with the idea of working in the fishhouse but her mother was still adamant that it was not a suitable job for her. She tried getting her father to intercede for her – no joy. Margaret decided to defy her mother.

'One day, I went to see Mr Miller. There were two brothers who owned the business, Henry and James. James lived in Dockwray Square and Henry lived in Drummond Terrace, where Northumberland Park is now. They were two good bosses. Mind you, you had to do your work and be quick at it, but not neglectful.

Barrels of fish stacked up on the Fish Quay at North Shields c.1900.

'Anyway, they had a little shop selling kippers which was kept by their sister, Hannah Miller. I went in there and asked if there was any vacancies for learners and she said that I had to see one of her brothers, but to wait because they wouldn't be long.

'Now I can't quite remember which one it was, Mr James, I think, and without hesitation he looked at me and said "Yes. We'll supply you with an oily [oilskin] and rubber boots. Start at 8 a.m. tomorrow."

'I was overjoyed, but I still had to tell my mother. Nervously, I said I was starting a new job. She asked where. And do you know, she just said, "What d'you want to do that for? You'll regret it." But I think she knew I was determined, because in the fishhouse in those days, everybody wore a three-cornered shawl wrapped across their chests to keep them warm and mother got hers out for me and gave it to me.

'By, but your hands got bitterly cold at first. They'd be dead white and numb. Then you'd get keens [tiny cuts] all over them and they'd get filled with salt and sting badly, or you'd get those tiny herring bones stuck in your fingers.

Women from a slightly earlier era than Margaret Compson sort herrings at the Fish Quay around 1898.

'Anyway, my first job was to prick on [scraping the scales and removing the head of the fish before it was gutted]. Mr James watched me for a few days and then asked if I'd done the work before, because he'd timed me and I was too fast for a beginner. I told him I'd seen it done many times and knew what was needed.

'Well, we worked ordinary hours through the week and Saturday 6 a.m. to 10 p.m. to cope with the glut – you'd get a bigger pay packet the week after – 17s 6d for 80 hours – but I wasn't allowed to start until 8 a.m. because I was too young. Anyway, after a while, I was sent to making boxes: eight nails, base on bench, two thick ends, four other pieces. Pick up all eight nails, make the box, and if a nail came through, start all over again.

'Then I became old enough to work from 6 a.m. and I was sent to collect smoking chips [oak shavings]. We had a big van and we'd get 50 bags on and off the back. Then, finally, I got to splitting herring: Mr James was so impressed at the pace I made that he put me up to being a "full woman" in a very short time. My first wage packet on that job was three, crisp, new ten shilling notes. Of course I gave it straight to my mother. But now I was a "full woman" and earning the wage, I asked for, and got, pocket money. Two shillings and sixpence a week – and, oh, what a lot I did with that half crown: You could go to the pictures for twopence, have a bag of broken biscuits for another twopence and then come out and go to Newton's for a penny saveloy.

'I've worked all my life. I went back to work the day after I was married – no honeymoons then. Then three months after my first son, Chris, was born I went back to work 'cos we needed the money for our own place. My mother looked after the baby and would bring him down to the fish house. Mr Miller would put a chair in the smokeroom and I'd feed the baby in there. Then my husband, Chris, got called up during the war. I moved back to Mam's and every night we'd go down to the shelter, but one night I wouldn't go to the one we always used, I was too frightened; my mother got furious with me. Instead, we went down to the one in our yard which had no roof on it. We were showered in glass because four bombs fell on Wilkinson's pop factory in Church Street that night [3 May 1941. Ninety-six people were killed and a further seven died from their injuries]. Chris got compassionate leave for that because our names were posted in the police station – they didn't know we'd not used the normal shelter under Wilkinson's factory, but if we had, we'd have been dead for sure. That's where the all the machinery landed in the shelter: nearly everyone was dead.

'Later, Chris, was posted missing in Burma. Everyone kept telling me to accept that he was dead, they even tried to make me take a widow's pension. I could see people thought I'd lost my reason when I refused to have it. Instead, I took a job at Tyne Meats, but I scandalised my mother and everybody else by refusing to wear black; in the end, I had to agree to wear navy, so people wouldn't talk. I just knew he wasn't dead. I knew inside that he was still alive. Mind you, I was among the last of the wives to know their husband had survived, and I was beginning to doubt myself by then. Chris finally came home to us in 1946, weighing only five stones. They told us we'd have no more children, but they were wrong. We had two more sons after he came back.

'I've worked all me life and enjoyed meself too, but if I never did another hand's turn, I would still think I'd done my fair share of work.'

The bus driver

'Work was so scarce you either did what you were asked or you were finished.'

Robbie McKenna of Coldrife was a modern young man and dreamed of driving motor vehicles. His school career had been disappointing, 'I had a chap called Barker sitting next to me, so I copied off him. Hopeless I was, especially at arithmetic.'

Rob's first paying job was as a stonebreaker: 'The roads were rough then. You'd have piles of rocks to break up into much smaller stones for filling in the potholes. Then the other men would come along, fill up the holes with the stones I'd bashed to bits and fix them into place with pitch.'

Soon though, life was to change as tragedy hit the family. Rob's father, a stone-mason, became ill and was hospitalised in Ashington.

'I walked the five miles into Rothbury to seek Dr Hedley and he came and said Dad had to go into hospital. I had a married sister in Ashington and we went to stay with her while he was in. He had a colostomy and almost died then. He was given two and a half years to live. Dr Muir at Ashington said to my mother, "What I'd do if I had what Mr McKenna has is to get a crate of whisky, take it up to ma bed and drink mysel' to death. He's a big, strong man and could last out two years or more of horrible suffering."

'It was awful. The [colostomy] bag had to be cleaned out each day and the smell was unbelievable. The worst part was that he knew everything that was happening to him, poor

Ashington Infirmary around 1920.

74

man. Mother scraped together enough money to buy a house in Ashington, to be near him. How she did it, I'll never know.

'The house in Coldrife stood completely empty then, even after the end of the war [World War One]. Stones got taken from it and none of the family asked what had happened to the house, even though we'd loved it. From it, we could see ships making their way up the coast and the heat haze rising on Simonside on hot days. Sun would glitter on the bright sea and purple heather would haze the hills. I dearly loved those hills and when I was older I'd often walk twenty miles or more over them on my day off. So there I was in grimy Ashington, standing gazing at the Simonside Hills and wishing I was there on them.

'The war had just finished and the soldiers were returning and, God knows, there was little enough to return to. You'd get colonels, majors, the lot, knocking on doors begging for a penny or two, or some odd jobs to do to earn them. Some had just been demobbed in France. Ex-servicemen often thought they'd been done out of jobs which should have been theirs, so you had to be careful when talking to them.

'I decided I was going to drive. I saw this advert for Welch's Sweets; they were looking for a young trainee salesman. I applied for it and Mr Welch himself took me round, showed me what to do. Step one: load up the van, travel all over the area. Of course, first of all I had to teach myself to drive the van – but I didn't tell him that. Step two: go out and sell; earn 5 per cent on all sales.

I was so shy, I was useless. After a month I had sold

nothing. Mr Welch came out with me again and I watched as he went in to the shopkeepers and talked them into buying everything. He had a real way with him, he could talk about the weather, their wives and families, the situation of the country. I do remember that toffee in the tray was new then. I couldn't shift it, but it practically walked out of the van for Mr Welch. I got a bit better,

An early Newcastle bus c.1912.

but I was never as good as him. He was a real salesman, I was just a clodhopper of a boy who drove a van and sold sweets.

'I'd set my sights though on working for United Buses, but I was too young to get a job with them – you had to be 21. When I was nineteen I got a job with a private carrier. I'd drive the small buses from Blyth to Ashington on the afternoon shift; sometimes, when we got back after the shift, there'd be a private carrier job to do which might take you until 10 or 12 at night. I was supposed to get a bonus, but I don't think I ever did. Work was so scarce, you either did what was asked or you were finished – there were plenty to take your place. Once I refused to work seven days a week and I was sacked. The Dole (Unemployment Benefit) was 18s per week but the Dole Office refused to give it to me because I'd been sacked. Eventually I got the money when they finally accepted the injustice of the circumstances, but it took some argument. Finally, my 21st birthday arrived and I was at last able to take the stiff test required for a bus driver.

'Remember that in the 1920s buses had solid tyres and carbide lamps with a fixed drum. Each evening you went down to stores to get your carbide, then you'd turn a little cap which dropped water onto the carbide and made the gas which you'd light. We also had two lights on the upper deck too, the conductress usually saw to them. At the end of each shift there'd be a kit inspection. Everything had to be in place, or you would be fined.

'Probably the most dangerous part of the job was starting the engine. We had huge starting handles and all engines had their idiosyncrasies; some were well-retarded. We had long pipes we fastened on to the handles and you'd have to be really careful with the compression of the charging gas in the cylinder heads. If the gas didn't fire, it could kick you back 20 yards or more. I remember these three young fellas coming during the Miners' Strike of 1926. They were desperate to earn a few extra pennies for their families and grabbed hold of the pipe. They were strong men, used to hard work. Two of them grabbed hold of the pipe, but it didn't fire. It threw them, but the other man was hit by the huge starting handle: it hit him in the jaw, caved in his chest and killed him. Poor fellow, he'd come in to earn a shilling and was killed.

'There was great competition between the bus companies. Often, the ex-servicemen would start up small companies with their gratuities and United would wait until they'd built up a profitable route and then buy them out. They did long-distance buses from Ashington to London in those days too. Lots of young girls were in service down there and would come home once a month or so. I was unsuited to the long journeys, they made me ill.

'Usually, I drove the Ashington to Cambois chain-ferry route. Your passengers were regulars and you got to know people, learned about their jobs, families and such like. I enjoyed it mostly and did it until World War Two. I left to become a tanker driver just a week before bus driving became a reserved occupation – which made my boss mad, as he'd tried to stop me from going.

'So it was off to Norwich, where I drove petrol tankers on a twelve hours on twelve hours off basis. It was a tremendous change – all that flat countryside after the hills of Northumberland. I'd be back here for every holiday.

'When I retired, I couldn't wait to return, I missed the hills so much. I still go out walking, but go nowhere near as far as I used to. I think, though, I could probably give you the name of every rock on Simonside, I'm that familiar with them. Come to think of it, I could probably do the same with the route from Ashington to Cambois, although I expect that's changed quite a bit by now.'

A Newcastle single-decker bus, 1925.

In service

'The mistress would say,
"I don't know what servants want wages for."'

While the young men looked around for any work that was available and only few found that they could enter the traditional occupations, the young women of the county in the 1920s had even less choice; many still went into domestic service. Among the women, there was a strict hierarchy in relation to being 'in service'. At the top of this came the governess; after her came the housekeeper and/or cook, then the lady's maid and nanny followed by the nursery maids, housemaids and, finally, the laundry maids and scullery maids. At the very bottom was the farm servant who required little refinement to do her work. 'Better class' servants tended to scorn farm servants.

Domestic Service Agencies were common and saved employers the trouble of vetting the young women themselves.

Barbara Coulthard, a miner's daughter of Pegswood, registered with an agency, 'They came and saw you in your own home, estimated what sort of family you came from, before setting you on.'

At the age of 16, having stayed at home to help her mother with the younger children (a very common practice with daughters), Barbara became a housemaid in Gosforth (a

Advertisement for domestic servants in a 1934 Newcastle Journal.

Domestic Servants

SITUATIONS VACANT

COOK and Housemaid Wanted; young; best part Gosforth; wireless; real home.—Write Box 50, Journal Office. 4965

COOK-GENERAL and Housemaid Required about 20th; must be competent; Jesmond.—Write Box 113, Journal Office. D.240

COMPANION-HOUSEKEEPER Required for Two Ladies living at Coast; maid kept.—Apply, with recent references, by letter only to Mrs A. F. Wilson. "Wayside," Axwell Park, Blaydon-on-Tyne. D.271

EXPERIENCED Housemaid, over 25, Wanted immediately; good needlewoman.—Woodslea, Clayton Road, Jesmond. 4969

GENERAL: Thoroughly experienced; over 25; plain cook, all duties; small modern house; good outings; two adults and young baby; references; uniform; comfortable home; state wage.—Write Box 59, Journal Office. D.303

GENTLEWOMAN (age 40 to 45) Required as Nurse-Companion to elderly lady (not invalid); country North Northumberland; maids kept.—Write fully, stating age, qualifications, and salary required, Box N.345, Journal Office. 4905

HOUSE-PARLOURMAID, reliable, age about 30, for South of England.—Write Box 17, Journal Office. D.309

HOUSE-PARLOURMAID Wanted; age between 21-30; good references.—Apply Mrs Richardson, Cliffe. Corbridge-on-Tyne. 4228 well-to-do suburb of Newcastle) for the princely sum of six shillings a week. Later, her sister joined her in the same household.

'It was a huge house and the mistress was very mean. My sister and I would take it in turns to ask for our money each week. She would look down her nose at us and say, "I don't know what servants want wages for, everything they need has already been given to them." In the end, my sister and I left when the household was broken up – the woman's husband left her – oh, it was all a dreadful scandal.

'After that I went to work in Corbridge; again as a housemaid. This house had a living room, a drawing room, a dining room, six bedrooms, kitchen, scullery and cold room. The laundry was sent out to be done. I was expected to wait at table, wash the glasses and see to visitors and their needs. Each morning the mistress would come into the kitchen and dish out all the supplies for the day; as much food as was needed for the whole household, including the staff. Now that wasn't considered mean, rather, in those days, it was called good housekeeping.

'In the morning, I wore a lavender uniform, but after lunch it was a black dress and white apron and cap.

'The master was a poultry farmer; the mistress went riding four times a week. They kept a nanny, a cook and me – the parlour-maid. In Corbridge I earned 11 shillings a week before I left. I kept in touch with the nanny after I was married. I was really sad to learn that the lady of the house had gone to South Africa to visit her husband's relatives and while she was there the Second World War was declared. She was allowed to bring home one child, so she brought home the elder boy. She went back to get the younger child and on the way home again the ship was torpedoed and they were both lost. The elder boy was later killed in the war.'

Elizabeth Ann Luck began as a nursemaid to Mr and Mrs Ferguson of Montague Avenue, in Gosforth. She got her job through the Girls' Friendly Society. Her duties included looking after the children, waiting at table and light housework. When the eldest child was taken into hospital to have his tonsils removed, it was Elizabeth Ann who went along with him. She was paid 8s 6d per week. Later, she improved her status by going to work as a cook for the Beavan family – Beavans was a large department store in Byker, Newcastle.

As a cook, she would be up by 7 a.m. to check that the fire was going strongly and would then begin breakfast –

bacon, eggs, fried bread, sometimes pancakes, occasionally kippers. Lunch would be something light: soup, followed by cutlets. The afternoon would then be spent baking scones and cakes and preparing the more substantial four course evening meal. The family consisted of Mr and Mrs Henry Beavan, and sons Mr Frank and Mr Fred – the latter lived at Whittingham and his mother would often spend a month visiting him. The family also had two daughters, both of whom married into the Fenwick family which also owned a department store.

Elizabeth recalls that Mrs Beavan had a superb head of hair and loved to have *eau de cologne* rubbed into it.

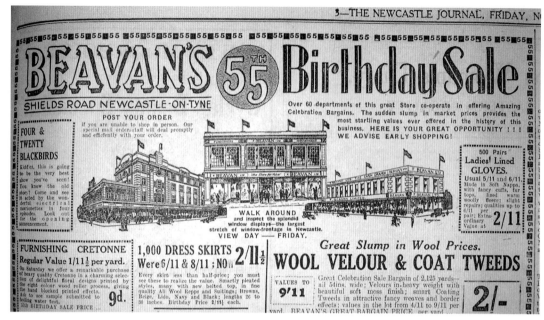

Beavan's advertises in November 1930.

She also remembers the many polite little notes, containing instructions, which would be passed to her: some requests, some suggestions and many compliments on the meals. She still has the handwritten recipe book given to her by Mrs Beavan, which details the family's preferences and dislikes.

Ada Foggin, whose pitman father had deserted the family and absconded to Australia, also became a housemaid, beginning work at James' farm in Wylam, where her mother was cook. One night, cutting through the farmyard, she heard noises in the barn. Peeping her head in, there was the sound of rustling, but nothing to be seen. Afraid, she ran back to the house and reported this to her mother. The following morning, they heard that two men from a Russian ship had been taken into custody and Ada remains convinced that they had taken refuge in the barn and she'd disturbed them. 'Of course, everyone called them spies, but I don't know if they were.'

Ada loved seeing to the hens; however, since she was the housemaid, Mrs James preferred her to stay indoors. She also tells the story of her first oyster, 'Mrs James was having a party and had ordered fresh oysters. The others all dared me to eat one – I'd never tasted them before – and that night, when they were served, Mrs J. wanted to know why one was missing. They had to tell her it had gone off, otherwise she'd have sacked me.'

Mollie Charlton, born in Newcastle in 1914, a tram driver's daughter, began work in a laundry but soon went into service. 'I saw an advert in *The Journal* offering a housekeeper's post in London, so I applied and got it. The man I went to work for was a film producer. He lived in a big house in Hampstead with his two sisters. I had my own room – the biggest room I've ever had. They were Jewish, and everything had to be kosher, so I had to learn to do things very differently in the kitchen. I was paid well, and I'd also get tickets to the cinema, so I saw all the latest films. I came home when my fiancé's mother fell ill and went to look after her. But, oh, how I missed London and the life I'd had.'

May Douglas had an aunt who had been a bondager so May was reluctant to work on the land, 'I wouldn't even pick a potato'. After several short-lived jobs in local shops from the age of 14 to 16, May finally went into service as a maid for one of the daughters of a family she'd known all her life. Shop work had paid her 7s 6d per week; in service she earned ten shillings. She was finally rescued from servitude by the Second World War when she was called up to become a fitter.

Some young women had rougher times than others. Mrs Robinson, born in Choppington in 1918, entered service in a household in Harrogate when she was fourteen. Two years later, homesick for the North-East, she got a job in Whitley Bay. Her delight at being back lasted only a very short time. Not surprising when she was paid a mere 7s 6d per week for washing, baking, cooking and cleaning. 'I was just a slave to them,' she says. She left and went to work at Choppington brickworks.

'It wasn't an easy time to find work [1934] and it wasn't what I'd really have chosen, but needs must. It was hard, manual labour. We earned twopence-halfpenny per 1000 bricks. There were great, massive drying sheds with iron floors. The clay would come down and whoever was on the barrow would have to throw this big handle to cut the clay. Then we'd have to lift the boards – there were four of them, with 15 or 16 bricks to the board – and stack them in the drying shed, before they went in the kilns. It was dirty work too, but you could earn 32s a week and that was excellent money for a woman in the mid-1930s.'

Margaret Douglas became a pupil teacher in 1918 and was paid 3s 6d per week. After working in the classroom for one year, she went off to Derby Training College for a further two years. She chose Derby, rather than Ripon or Durham where she also been granted places, only because it meant a long train journey and Margaret was to become a keen traveller, eventually taking a year's unpaid leave from work in order to travel around the world. At Derby College 'freshers' were given someone from the senior year to look after them, often resulting in lifelong friendships – as in Miss Douglas's case. Her mentor emigrated to Canada and the two women visited each other frequently.

On graduation, Margaret took up a post in a Morpeth school where her wage as a qualified teacher was £11 per month. Her annual problem was that His Majesty's Inspectors of Schools visited every year in mid-May. As Miss Douglas points out: 'Flitting Day was May 12th, so every year they would come along and we'd have all these children who barely knew the school or its teachers, never mind what we'd taught.'

Meanwhile, Mrs Bolam returned to Alnwick from her finishing school to a leisurely life of tennis parties, country walks and picnics. In winter there were house parties. In many ways her life resembled those of Jane Austen's female characters. In fact, she dearly longed to become a nurse, but this was considered a totally unsuitable occupation for a woman of her class. Her only chance to experience anything of life in a medical environment was to serve as a VAD in a little cottage hospital during World War Two. She still recalls the excitement of attending two births.

In Wooler, Mildred Wright's mother, as the wife of a bank manager, insisted that her daughters learn to keep a decent household. Although her girls did not go out to work, they rose at six each morning and were taught to cook and bake.

Mildred says: 'We had lots of important customers at the bank in Wooler and Daddy would bring them through to the guest room where we would serve them with tea and cake. I would also be expected to play the piano. There were dinner parties and mother made sure we knew an admirable table when we saw it.'

The greatest adventure of Mildred's youth happened when Thomas Hedley, the soap manufacturer, was taken over by Proctor and Gamble, the American conglomerate. She became the companion of one of the young American wives for six months: 'I went to Benton and I had a wonderful time. Nowadays there is no class system, not at all like it was when I was a girl – a good thing too – but I think my American friend was the first to make me sensitive to how class-ridden and hierarchical our society was and it changed me.'

The privileged world of the middle-class. Top, a bank in Wooler (though not the British Linen Bank), and below, a tennis party around 1930.

82

Stepping out

'Crowds of us went out together.
We had Sunday School trips and charabanc outings.'

There were no 'teenagers' in the early years of the 20th century; instead, there were young workers, almost all of whom were already contributing to the family income. The amount they contributed might be small, but as a proportion of the total income of that family it was significant.

A few, like Margaret Douglas, Mrs Buglass, Olive Purves, Mildred Wright or Mr Price enjoyed secondary education. Mr Price, for instance, took up a scholarship to Duchess School, Alnwick, but after matriculating at sixteen he discovered that all that was available to a boy with a school certificate but no influential friends was work as a Railway Clerk. He chose, instead, to join his father on the farm, 'I couldn't bear to work indoors, so I went to work for my father. I'd been helping out on the farm anyway since I was a little lad.'

Adolescence was regarded as that awkward phase between childhood and adulthood during which one matured and ended up taking complete emotional and financial responsibility for oneself. It was also a time of growing freedom to pursue one's own interests.

What did these young people do with their precious leisure hours? In many ways this depended on when they were born. Those born pre-1910 spent their leisure in much the same way as had their parents: as members of church groups they cycled, went off on organised rambles and played tennis. May Telfer recalled fern-collecting outings: 'People

Excursions by charabanc for workers or church groups were a treat during the summer.

were very keen on ferns those days. In winter, we'd spend time identifying and pressing the collections. Then, sometimes, there'd be magic lantern shows or talks from people who had done interesting work with the missions. There was also the church choir, or the Sunday School. The church was such a large part of our lives.'

Barbara Coulthard met her husband through the church. 'There were crowds of us went out together. We had Sunday School trips and charabanc outings. One of my friends was mad for this boy and asked me to find out if he was going on the Sunday School trip, so I did. He answered that he'd only go if I was going and then my sister went and told my friend what he'd said and she was mad with me about it!'

A day at the seaside around 1930.

For those born post-1910, however, a new, modern world of entertainment became available. The phonograph supplanted the piano and, most importantly, the movies, known as 'The Pictures', had arrived, albeit with captions to read instead of voices and sound effects.

Mr Robinson recalls 'Pop Thompson' who owned a soft drinks, or 'pop', factory in Rothbury: 'Oh, he was marvellous on the violin when he accompanied the film. He could express any emotion: fear, horror, excitement, tension, laughter, mischief, love, sadness or pathos. Eh, the audience would be crying with laughter, or wiping away tears of sorrow while they watched. Oh, yes, he could really get them going. And d'you know what? Pop Thompson only ever played one tune:

Hey Diddle Diddle!'.

Mr Robinson remembers the picture show and the dance which followed cost 6d. 'We'd help set up the hall in the afternoon: scrub the floors, set up the chairs. Not once did Pop Thompson offer us a discount for helping him to get the place ready.'

Ned Thompson, a miner's son from East Chevington (no relation of Pop Thompson) recalls the Red Row Picture House which originally belonged to Jack Bell. Ned recalls that the first talking picture was 'Ben Hur' and that Billy Mavin of Amble was the last projectionist at the cinema before it closed in the mid-1960s. The old cinema building is

The Picture Hall, Red Row, near Amble. It closed in 1963.

house at the Albion Cinema, North Shields, with her boyfriend, Chris (later to be her husband) and her workmate, Sarah.

'First though, Sarah and me would go to Holmes' sweet shop and buy broken chocolates for 2d. Chris would have stood in line to keep our place for two hours so we could get in to see the picture. It cost us 3d to get in.

'Then there was the dancing. Unfortunately, Chris didn't dance and I was mad for it. I've seen me finish a late shift and rush up to Pearlies Dance Hall, still dressed in my oily to have the last dance.'

Betsy Simpson recollects the Harmony Cinema in the town. Most of all though, she remembers the dance halls, particularly the Princess Ballroom (gutted by fire on April 4th, 1944).

For the much younger Jimmy Ditchburn, the Princess Ballroom in Ashington fuelled his new passion; although he

now Pettica's Garage. As a youth, Ned, too, had spent some time as a projectionist at the Picture House and remembers that a girl from Kellet's, the sweet shop next-door, used to come in during the intervals to sell penny chocolate bars. The pianist who accompanied the film in the days before the 'talkies' was Rachel Johnstone. Before the Picture House was established, there were travelling shows. Ned remembers that a projectionist would turn up at the local hall, hang up a large white sheet and set out chairs. The equipment would be placed on an upturned pigeon cree and the audience would flood in to see Laurel and Hardy or Charlie Chaplin.

Margaret Compson, the fish gutter from North Shields, worked Saturday shifts which ended late, but she received special permission from her parents to attend the second

HARBOTTLE

Shepherds' Dance.—Another impromptu dance was held in Alwinton to give a fillip to the Alwinton Border Shepherds' Show, to be held on the 17th of this month. It was not advertised, but as in the "Lady of the Lake" the fiery cross went flying through the hills. The shepherds flocked in and tested the capacity of the granary of the Red Lion to the utmost for their beloved show, of which they are immensely proud. Foggin's band kept them moving with some swing, and the new secretary, Mr W. Dagg, helped to make it a big success.

A dance at Harbottle is reported in a 1934 Newcastle Journal.

could no longer compete in cross country runs or sprints after the damage to his knee in his first week at the pit, he could dance, and dance he did!

Mildred Wright in Wooler enjoyed the rather more staid dances held at the Archbold Hall in the town and was to meet her husband there.

Ned Thompson enthuses about the wonderful sprung floor of the Central Hall above the Co-op store in nearby Widdrington and also recollects dances at the Primrose Dance Hall in Red Row.

Lizzie Voersing remembers the colliery dances, the church hall dances and the Co-op dances to which everyone in Newbiggin went.

Most of the married contributors born before 1910 met their spouses on church outings, those born post 1910 met their husbands or wives either through friends with whom they went dancing, or at the dance hall.

A somewhat formal occasion! The Farmers' Ball, Newcastle, 1930.

Betsy Simpson says: 'I met my husband when I was only sixteen. I used to go dancing [in the Princess Ballroom] with a group of young people and his sister was one of them. When I'd call for her, he would disappear into the back room because he didn't dance and his sister used to say, "Our Jack wants to take you to the pictures, Betsy." I was quite happy the way I was, but they persuaded me to make up a foursome and two years later Jack and me got married in Lynemouth church – we were the first couple to be married there. I wore a suit I'd made myself.'

Mrs Bolam of Alnwick also met her husband at a dance.

'We used to go out with a group of friends. He fell for me and I fell for him. He was not the sort of person I planned to marry, nor was he at all the sort my mother had in mind for me. Both he and his father were land agents and chartered surveyors in Berwick. He wasn't earning much then and he was ten years older than me. We were engaged for four years – much too long, but I rather think my mother hoped the engagement would fail – before we married at St Michael's Church in Alnwick. I wore a cream satin dress and a Brussels lace veil – I didn't want to wear my mother's wedding dress, but my daughter was married in it.'

Mildred Wright also had difficulty in persuading her parents that her choice was a suitable match.

'I met Jim [a plumber] at a dance in Wooler. When it came to the Ladies' Choice, there were four visitors and Jim was the first one I came to. I hoped that he'd walk me home, but he didn't even ask. Then he began to cycle from Newcastle to Wooler each Saturday night [a distance of 46 miles]. He'd say that as he came up the rise to Cowgate [a suburb of Newcastle] he would see the Cheviot Hills and think of me. We went out for six months before we even held hands. Other boys would come and ask to take me out and father would see them off, but Jim persisted and refused to be sent away.

'Father was much older than Mother – very Victorian in his attitudes – and I think he believed that I ought to have the steadiness of an older man. He arranged for me to go out with one of the Bank's inspectors. The man was as bald as a coot, but father insisted I should go. Unfortunately, the man was a bit fast and took liberties. I couldn't possibly tell father what he was doing, we just hadn't the words to discuss it then. I had to say that I couldn't bear bald men which made Father think I was even more of a flibberti-gibbet than he'd believed.

'Jim had been coming for four years; Father refused to relent and would not give his permission for us to court formally. Jim told my father he intended to buy me a ring for my 21st birthday and Father was not

happy; he still would not give us his blessing. Jim and I eloped. I never fell out with my parents, but they didn't come to the wedding. Jim's sister took me in until we were married.

'It was only a couple of years later, when my son was born, that Father just walked in to my house and said, "Is this my grandson?" Later, when my daughter was born, my father was entranced by her. He died when she was just two-and-a-half years old. He was 70 years of age.' (Jim Wright proved to be as determined a businessman as he was a courting man and eventually ran a well-known plumber's merchant business. Mildred's father could not have wished for a better, more successful husband for his daughter.)

'I think what I remember most is how absolutely innocent we were at that time. If, as an adult, you should happen to

The St James Cycling Club, Newcastle, around 1930. People thought nothing of a long cycle ride to see friends.

see a pregnant lady, you turned your eyes away. As children, we had no idea of how babies arrived. Even after I was married, I wasn't entirely sure.'

This absolute innocence is confirmed by all the women. Betsy Simpson, married at eighteen to a twenty-year-old miner, recalls that neither she nor her new husband had any idea of what marriage was about. 'Green as grass!' she laughs, 'It took us two weeks to find out. And then I fell with my first son, but we didn't know how to tell the parents, because then they'd know we'd been doing it!'

Even Margaret Compson, born a little later in 1918, confirms, 'Oh, we hadn't the words. You wouldn't have known who or how to ask. I had a lovely wedding – a pink satin dress and two bridesmaids – and we hired Pearlies Hall for the reception. I fell with young Chris straight away. I'd no idea how long the pregnancy would take, and even when I was six or seven months I still didn't know where babies came from. My mother didn't tell me a thing. When my waters broke, I thought that was it – the labour, that is. My neighbour came in. I said to her, "I hope they don't stitch me up. I don't fancy a line down my belly". Well, she was puzzled, but I thought they'd have to cut me open to get the baby out. It was a bit of a surprise when I discovered how he came.'

Mrs May Telfer was the first to mention the 'golden scissors' which many women believed the doctor would use to cut open the abdomen and deliver the baby. She began by telling of her wedding preparations: 'My bridesmaid and I got on our bicycles and rode to Berwick to look for dresses. We couldn't find anything, so it was back to North Sunderland with empty arms. The following week, we set out on our bikes for Newcastle. Now you have to remember that this was on unmetalled roads, which were full of potholes, and the distance would be, oh, at least fifty miles, I suppose. By the time we got there, we were exhausted. We were staying overnight with an aunt and uncle of mine and they insisted that the following day we do our shopping then they'd put us on the train back. We both found what we wanted and I was married in a beautiful blue satin dress.

'Of course, no-one had told me anything about childbirth. When I'd been little, I'd watch the doctor coming and going when my brothers were born and I'd complain he never brought me a sister in his bag. We believed then that babies were brought in the doctor's black bag and he brought them from Holy Island. Later, after I was married, I heard rumours of the 'golden scissors' which the doctor used. I wasn't sure what to believe, but there was no one with whom I could decently discuss it. We were so innocent in those days.'

Mrs Sparke, Mrs Turnbull, Mrs Wood and Mrs Compson were among those who had also heard of the golden scissors. They covered a geographical spread from Allendale in the south-west of Northumberland, Tynedale in the west, and

Blyth and North Shields in the south east coastal area. Given that Mrs Telfer hailed from the far northern end of Northumberland, this suggests that it was a county-wide myth.

Mrs Telfer's reference to both decency and innocence underlies the problem. To protect their innocence, no-one told the young women anything; however, if they wished to retain their decency, they were unable to ask. Mrs Sparke, for instance, recalls delicately approaching an older sister to ask about the 'golden scissors' and having the whole business of being cut open by them solemnly confirmed.

Mrs Bolam is of the opinion that young women were kept in ignorance rather than in innocence. 'Most of us were not given the vocabulary to discuss intimate matters and I am certain it must have resulted in much harm for many women.'

Before marriage, Mrs Bolam had dared to ask her fiancé about the physical side of marriage. 'My mother told me nothing, not even the night before we were married. I was curious and Robert and I were in love and when you're in love things do happen. Robert gently explained it all to me. The following afternoon, I went for a walk with a friend of mine – the doctor's daughter – and couldn't wait to tell her all. When I'd finished, she simply gave me a very odd look and seemed rather taken aback that I hadn't known all this before. Do remember that I was 24 when I married, hardly a child. My friend did, however, confirm everything Robert had told me.'

All of the women were determined that their own children should be better prepared to deal with intimate matters and that 'not having the words for it' should not be a problem for them. Hence, the myth of the golden scissors seems to have died out by 1950. Having said that, many men and women who grew up immediately after World War Two would still have had difficulty in speaking of both intimate body parts and sexual matters because they had not been given the language to discuss such things. In this matter of innocence and experience, the end of the 20th century could not be more different than the beginning of the century.

Before going on to talk of children and families, I would like to mention a couple of Northumbrian wedding customs. A few contributors mentioned that before they were allowed through the church gates, they were expected to pay a 'ransom' to the local children. Another custom, more common in the west of the county, was that of 'walking on gold', which meant the bride wore a gold sovereign inside her shoe. This lasted until late in the 20th century, although I suspect that sovereigns were in rather short supply by the 1980s and the 'sovereign' became a £1 coin. Until relatively recently, readers of the *Hexham Courant* were extremely familiar with the headline, 'Bride Walked on Gold'.

More common though, and a custom which also lasted well into the 20th century, was that of the 'Hoyin' Oot'. The 'Hoyin' Oot' (or Throwing Out, for those unfamiliar with the dialect) was the custom of the bridegroom throwing handfuls of pennies as the couple left the church grounds. The custom had changed slightly in that originally the coins were warmed over lamps or candles and were hot when thrown. Local children supplemented their pocket money with these wedding pennies, although as Christopher Blandford says, 'Aw, hey, we hadn't a look in. We had to compete with the fisherwives in Newbiggin. After all, a penny was a penny and they saw no indignity at all in scrambling for money.'

Baby days

'Robbie McKenna's first clear memory is of wearing a dress.'

Today, many couples agonise over whether they should bring a child into the world at all. This would not have occurred to any of our forbears: marriage meant children; the lack of them could bring great unhappiness. It is worth pointing out that although contributors themselves frequently came from large families, none produced large families of their own. This is reflected in national statistics. In 1900 the fertility rate per woman was 3.5 children; by 1997 this had fallen to 1.7 children. Most of the married contributors had only two children.

The greatest change of all is, without a doubt, in our attitude towards single parenthood: it would not even have been considered as an option for three-quarters of the 20th century. Children born outside of marriage were not welcomed. Single mothers were regarded as 'fallen women' and were shunned by a more morally-hidebound society; in the early years of the century they were sometimes labelled as 'morally incompetent' and locked away in mental institutions for most of their lives. Illegitimate children were at considerable disadvantage, not just socially, but also legally: until the 1960s, legally-designated bastards were unable to take up company directorships; they were unable to inherit from their father's estate, even if legally acknowledged as his child, unless they were specifically included in his will.

The moral stigma attached to illegitimacy meant that in order to protect a family's reputation from 'what the neighbours would say' the single, pregnant woman was spirited away to stay with distant relatives or sent to an institution

which dealt with 'fallen women'. The great majority of babies born outside of marriage were promptly given up for adoption. Usually, the poor mother was not even allowed to see her child, on the grounds that it would awaken 'unnatural maternal feelings' in her. On the very rare occasions in which the child was kept, it often became subsumed within its grandparents' or an aunt's family and counted as one of their own. The natural mother was allowed to make no claim on the child. Much malicious counting on fingers was done when a child arrived within the first year of marriage; I suspect that this was a distorted reaction to that very innocence and ignorance referred to in the previous chapter. Certainly, there were many defensive references to 'honeymoon babies' among newly-wed wives who produced a child within nine or ten months.

Parents nowadays are aware that the birth of their first child changes their whole lifestyle and often requires a larger car, a larger bathroom and, preferably, a larger living space. Grandparents complain that visiting parents bring along with them a vanload of baby accoutrements, but this is a relatively recent phenomenon. What did expectant parents in the early part of the 20th century need to provide and how much would it all cost? The following is a list of minimum requirements for a layette made to be given to a 'necessitous woman' (i.e. poor women, but not an unmarried mother) by members of Embleton Women's Institute in the 1930s. Prices would have changed little in the decade :

4 Binders	@	-	-
4 Vests	@	1s	4s
24 Turkish Napkins	@	1s	24s
3 Pilchers	@	1s	2s
3 Flannel Napkins	@	1s 10d	5s 6d
3 Day Barracoats	@	3s 6d	10s 6d
3 Night Barracoats	@	3s 6d	10s 6d
2 Petticoats	@	3s 6d	7s 0d
3 Nightgowns	@	2s 6d	5s 0d
3 Day Coats	@	1s 0d	3s 0d
1 Head Shawl	@	3s 6d	3s 6d
2 Knitted Bootees	@	4d	8d
6 Bibs	@		4s 6d

Total Cost   £5. 0. 4d

This layette was the same whether for a boy or a girl. Small boys wore dresses until they were almost ready for school, at which time they were 'britched'. Stonemason's son, Rob McKenna's first clear memory is of wearing a dress and the inconvenience of it when playing in the mud.

The layette for the new baby would be in white, usually homemade by the expectant mother, and items would be lovingly trimmed with lace, swansdown and much complicated tucking, drawn-thread work, or dainty embroidery.

During pregnancy, the mother would have been expected to be discreet in allowing others to see her burgeoning state and would most probably have done her best to stay strictly within the family orbit for the final two months.

For a first child, the perambulator, preferably coach-built and therefore sprung, (and many former carriage builders went into producing prams as the motor car took over from the horse-drawn coach) would be bought well in advance but would not be delivered until a fortnight after the birth. There were two reasons for this custom: one being superstitious and the other entirely practical. The superstition related back to high child mortality rates of the early 19th century and the sense of tempting fate by having a pram in waiting. Often, when subsequent children were on the way, unless there was an infant already in the house using it, the perambulator would be temporarily removed as the birthdate approached.

The other reason for taking delivery of the pram after fourteen days was that until she was ready to be 'churched' the mother would stay indoors. Indeed, birthing practices insisted on a 'lying-in' period of 14 days, although many contributors claim to have ignored the latter instruction and got out of their beds considerably earlier.

Almost invariably, babies were born at home. The only exception I came across was the more affluent Mrs Bolam, by then a land agent's wife, whose husband insisted on her giving birth at the Rothbury Cottage Hospital with their local doctor in attendance. Cost, of course, was the major problem. The Northumberland Federation of Women's Institutes made an annual collection towards providing a bed and cot at Willington Quay Maternity Hospital, 'In order that no necessitous woman will be excluded merely on the grounds that she is unable to contribute a certain sum towards her cost of treatment.' After the National Health Service was set up in 1948, it slowly became much more usual for a woman

Beavans advertises its best prams, 1922.

to have their own GP delivering the child at a local maternity unit; pre-1948 this was a rare occurrence, but by the late 1950s it was common.

Naming the child was rather more simple than it is for today's parents. Nowadays, parents trawl through long lists and choose the names they like the sound of. They are also very careful about initials, trusting that they do not land their offspring with those such as JCB, DVD, VCR: a hopeless endeavour, given the pace of technological change.

In the past, it was customary to give family names and doubtless, in the future, modern names will cause enormous headaches for amateur genealogists who will have few clues as to which family line to pursue in tracing their forbears. May Telfer, herself a Mole before marriage, tells a story concerning of the Mole family of North Sunderland/Seahouses:

Three cousins were playing together when a stranger came into the village asking for directions to the house of William Mole. The three boys supplied them and the stranger, impressed at how polite they were, asked one of them, 'And what is your name, my little man?' He replied, 'Willie Mole, sir.' The stranger promptly turned to the second boy, 'And yours, little fellow?' 'Willie Mole, sir.' The stranger frowned but turned to the smallest boy, 'And I suppose you're going to tell me that you too are Willie Mole?' 'Yes, sir, that's my name.' Convinced that the boys were teasing him, the man turned away in annoyance, muttering, 'Is every man in this place called William Mole?' and went off to see William Mole, the grandfather of the three cousins, after whom each was named. In order to distinguish between them within the family, the three boys were known as 'Moses', 'Carrapah' and 'Widdie', but May has no idea why.

It was customary to give the first boy the name of the paternal grandfather and the first girl the name of her maternal grandmother. Another frequent custom in Northumberland was to name a second son with his mother's maiden name, resulting in names like Charlton Robson, Henderson Harding, Fenwick Armstrong, or Foster Davison, all familiar to the author. The name of the actor Robson Green, a Northumbrian, follows in this tradition, as does Charlton Heston, the movie star, whose mother, Lila, was a Northumbrian. The second son might also carry the name of his maternal grandfather, while a younger sister would be named for her paternal grandmother. After that, other family names might be used, although there are exceptions: Barbara Coulthard, the only girl in her family, is not aware of any other family member with her name. Minnie Craighead's mother, who had already lost four babies in infancy, would not give Minnie a name she had already used for a deceased child, although it certainly would not have been considered peculiar to do so.

And so to the christening of the new baby. Unlike today, when babies are often months old when baptised, this ceremony would take place within a relatively short time, for the mother would be 'churched' (a church ceremony of thanksgiving, blessing and purification after a birth). Once churched, she was considered acceptable to society once again. Churching, as a ceremony, was dropped by both Roman Catholic and the Anglican churches in the 1960s.

The baptismal ceremony itself remains much as it was, although the language used today is considerably less formal.

In Northumberland, baptism was an occasion for another tradition – the giving of the 'Almis' or christening piece.

The 'Almis' was small package usually containing salt, bread or cake, sugar, and a piece of silver. The salt symbolised savour in life; the bread or cake, sustenance; sugar, of course for sweetness; silver for prosperity. Having said that, I must admit that contributors did describe 'Almis' packages with different contents. Jimmy Ditchburn, for instance, remembers that in Ashington it contained 'Silver, salt, candle and cheese.' Whatever the other combinations, salt and silver part were always an important part of the Almis.

The Almis gift had to be given to the first child of the opposite sex met on the way to church. When given on the way, it indicated that the baby would have good fortune in life. In the event that no-one was met, it was possible to hand over the Almis after the baptism – again to someone of the opposite sex – but this was considered rather less auspicious for the child.

Mr Robinson, whose family eventually moved to Rothbury, remembers his mother giving him a good telling-off for not accepting the christening piece gift from a family on their way to the church:

'At the time, it was a real puzzle to me. I'd been warned over and over again never to accept anything from a stranger, and here I was being shouted at for not taking a parcel from folks I didn't know!'

Mrs Buglass recounts a charming tale concerning the Hall family of Beadnell Hall and the Almis gift:

'They'd had a little girl and were on their way to the church. Arrangements had been made that the cook's nephew would meet them on the way and they'd give him the christening piece. Well, he didn't turn up – later they learned that he'd gone down with chickenpox that morning. They met no-one on their way to Beadnell Church and May Hall got into a bit of a state, for it wasn't lucky to go into the church without having given over the gift. We were all sent searching for a boy. Then I discovered this young gentleman looking around the church. He was well-dressed and seemed like a wealthy person to me, but he was obviously still quite young, so I approached him. It turned out he was a law student at Oxford or Cambridge and just visiting Beadnell. He was bemused when I explained the problem but agreed to

Beadnell Hall c.1900.

come and meet the Halls. They handed over the christening piece to him, explaining its special significance. I'm sure he thought we were all very quaint.

'Years later, when her daughter was getting married, May Hall thought it might be a nice idea to send him an invitation to the wedding. She spent months tracking him down; how she managed it, I don't know. Finally, she sent off the invitation and he accepted. It turned out that he'd become a solicitor in Brighton. He came to the wedding and he brought a gift for the bride: the very same silver shilling he'd got in the christening piece. He'd kept it all those years and he gave it back to her to be used for her first child's christening.'

Traditions

'There'd be a clothes basket filled with eggs, some boiled
and dyed them, but mostly they were fresh.'

Traditional customs gave colour and savour to simple, hardworking lives. Some still live on, some have been rediscovered, others have died out in a more complicated world. Many of the customs were designed to ward off bad luck and it is easy to see how important this must have been in times when people had little control over their own lives. Better health and education meant that superstitions were already losing their power at the turn of the 19th and beginning of the 20th century, yet enough uncertainty remained for some customs to continue. This chapter records some of the occasions throughout the year which were regarded as special.

New Year's Day: in Northumberland New Year was party time, and indeed still is. As in Scotland, as the clock approaches midnight, some poor dark-haired man is thrust out into the frosty night to 'first-foot'. This is a very ancient custom, probably dating from pagan times. The first-foot' must be male and dark-haired. Fair-haired males will stand out in the darkness, hence evil spirits may be drawn to them and they will bring ill luck into the house – although not nearly as much as a female first-footer, who will bring calamity with her.

The shivering first-foot will not be allowed back over the doorstep until the clock has finished striking midnight and he

will then be expected to bring with him a gift of coal (for warmth and human kindness), salt (to bring savour to the household) and coins (for prosperity). He'll be given food and drink, usually whisky, although in teetotal homes this might be tea. Having said this, my husband's former landlady – a staunch Methodist – always provided a glass of home-made wine, made with her own grapes, which she fondly, and merrily, imagined to be harmless for not a drop of alcohol had been added to it!

The town of Allendale in West Northumberland, still celebrates each New Year with the Burning of the Tar Barrels. Twenty-four quaintly-clad men with blackened faces, who are known as Guisers, are led by a band of musicians in a parade round the town. On their heads they carry blazing barrels of tar. At midnight the tar barrels are thrown on to the flaming bonfire in Allendale Market Place. Then people dance to the sound of the band that led the procession. The custom is said to date back to the Vikings who invaded Northumberland in the 8th century; or it may possibly relate to even earlier times. Certainly, there are strong echoes of a similar event which takes place in Lerwick in the Shetland Isles in which a Chief Guiser is elected each year to lead the New Year celebrations. The custom is particularly quaint in Northumberland in that it survives in an area with a strong

Noncomformist tradition.

It was also customary in Northumberland to 'Start the year anew.' This meant that housewives cleaned and scrubbed their houses on New Year's Eve and paid all outstanding bills so that the household might not be in debt for the rest of the year.

Twelfth Night, 6 January: the Christmas tree had to come down and all the decorations put away by the feast of The Epiphany which is the twelfth night of the Christmas season (the first night being the feast of St Stephen on Boxing Day). To leave any vestige of the Christmas celebrations on show was to invite bad luck into the house.

Shrove Tuesday: 'Always pancakes on Shrove Tuesday. At school, we were told that it was because in olden times they had to eat up all their eggs and meat which they weren't allowed for Lent.' (Mrs Hindmarsh, Alnwick, 1900, a hind's daughter).

Allendale, around 1920.

Her friend, Sally, from Chathill, also the daughter of a farmworker agreed: 'We were told that too. You know, come to think of it, mother never made pancakes at any other time. I've a feeling that because it was just before the beginning of Lent, she considered it unlucky to do it any other time.'

Mr Robinson, who grew up in Rothbury, remembers that there used to be a football game in the village on Shrove Tuesday which lasted from morning until twilight. This footballing custom survives in Alnwick.

Elisabeth Luck recalled Mothering Sunday (the fourth Sunday in Lent): 'Those of us in service were allowed to go home on Mothering Sunday. Only the girls though. The men and boys weren't allowed.'

Carlin Sunday (the 5th Sunday of Lent): 'Tid, Quid, Misere, Carlin, Palm and Paste Egg Day, that's what we used to recite to remember the Sundays of Lent, but I never really knew what it meant, except for the last three. Mam made carlins for us. They're black peas – well greyish-looking really – you boiled them first, then fried them in butter and served a dish of them sprinkled with a little sugar … When I went to London, where I was in service, they had never heard of carlins.' (Mollie Charlton)

A greengrocer's shop in Morpeth Market Place was still selling carlins in the 1980s. As an old custom it is pretty sensible, since by the 5th Sunday of Lent the fast would have resulted in depleted stores of protein in the body and all members of the pea family are reasonably high in protein. Mollie's description of the cooking procedure is reminiscent of Mexican refried beans.

Margaret Douglas remembered Good Friday: 'Everyone agreed that this was an extremely solemn day. 'We weren't allowed to play outside on any Sunday, it wasn't considered seemly. We went to church and to Sunday School, then we came home and read. Good Friday was like an even more strict Sunday. Bodens, the wet fish shop would be open for a couple of hours in the morning and there'd be queues snaking around the block. The Catholics had to eat fish every Friday, but on Good Friday, we all ate fish – always boiled and served with parsley sauce – for our meal, then there'd be church in the afternoon. A real pall of sadness would hang over Amble that day. Nowadays, there are shops open and people treat it as a holiday, but then it was a very solemn day.'

Easter Sunday: 'From after midday on Easter Saturday, we'd take our baskets and go visiting the big houses and farms. There'd be a wicker clothes basket filled with eggs out-side the gate. Some would boil them and dye them, but most were fresh.' (Mr Robinson)

'Oh, Easter was a lovely time. You all went out collecting eggs from the farms and then you'd bring them home to make them into paste eggs.' (May Telfer)

Paste eggs is the Northumbrian term for the original Easter eggs. These were boiled eggs, brightly dyed or painted, and decorated. The term 'paste' is said to be a corruption of the word 'Pasque' from the French, or 'Paschal' from the Latin.

Egg collecting.

May Douglas loved the duck eggs which were available from Coquet Island, particularly those of 'Cuddy's ducks', the eider ducks ('Cuddy' being a reference to St Cuthbert).

The custom of paste eggs survives into the 21st century. Northumbrian people still use traditional methods to colour their eggs: they boil them in onion skins, tea leaves or coffee grounds. Some create clever patterns by attaching fern leaves to the egg before dyeing, others get out their paints, felt pens, sequins and ribbons and decorate the egg artistically. In the many egg competitions which take place in towns and villages throughout the region, huge imagination is shown by children and adults.

Other customs concerning eggs and Easter also survive: 'japping' or 'jauping' is something akin to playing conkers, using raw eggs rather than horse chestnuts. Whoever is left with an intact egg is the winner: messy, but fun. Egg-rolling also takes place in some parts of the county. Morpethians, for example, will proudly tell incomers that however long they live in Morpeth they cannot be Morpethians until they have sledged down the Ha'a Hill on a tea tray or rolled their paste eggs down it on Easter Sunday.

Throughout March there would also have been the Hiring Fairs at Market towns throughout the county: Alnwick, Morpeth, Wooler, Hexham, Haltwhistle and Bellingham will all

have had their own Hirings. 'Flitting Day', as already mentioned, was on 12 May and this may have been a reason for the fact that there were no Whitsunday Walks, or processions, in the region as there were in Yorkshire and Lancashire, Contributors did mention, however, that Whitsunday was usually when they walked out in their new summer clothes. Until 1927, Stagshaw Fair, first held in 1204, took place at Stagshaw Bank, Corbridge, on the Saturday before Whitsunday. From Stagshaw, the stallholders, selling gingerbread and sweets, then moved to Rothley Village for a Whitsunday Fair on a Sunday, (most unusual), then on to

Morpeth from Ha'a Hill around 1900.

Rothbury for Whit Monday.

For those who lived closer to Newcastle, (known as 'The Toon') there were 'The Hoppings' – a very large fair which is still held during Race Week, the last full week in June, on the Town Moor (a large tract of land within the city boundaries which belongs to the Freemen of the City). Mollie Charlton comments on the rides such as the merry-go-rounds and shuggie boats. Then there were lots of freak shows: 'the bearded lady', 'the world's smallest man' or 'the human snake'; there were exhibition booths selling medicines guaranteed to cure even the most serious complaint. Where now there are vans selling hamburgers, hot dogs, candy floss or ice cream, then there were lines of stalls selling delicacies such as cowheel pies, pigs' trotters, or baked ham with pease pudding (a plate of yellow split peas) as well as cinder toffee and gingerbread stalls. Fortune tellers' caravans remain with us, no longer brightly-painted and drawn by a pony, but in smart steel and glass fibre and drawn by a SUV. They are parked well away from the technologically-controlled, complicated and heart-attack inducing rides.

Race Week was an important holiday in the town. The racecourse at Gosforth Park was always crowded during that last week in June, particularly for the running of the Northumberland Plate, also known as 'The Pitman's Derby'.

Fairs in general were held throughout the

Newcastle festivities: top, the Hoppings, Newcastle, 1938, and below, crowds at the Northumberland Plate, Gosforth, 1952.

county in July and August. Margaret Douglas recalls the Amble Feast: 'It was held on August Bank Holiday Monday which was at the beginning, rather than the end of August then. It was always at the bottom of Queen Street. Murphy's switchback used to come and you'd get free rides if you were on it first. When we [Margaret and her twin sister, Issie] got older, the great thing was to go home for supper and then come back about 9 p.m. when it was getting dark and all the lights would begin to glow.

'Dad always knocked a coconut off the shy – he'd a good eye – and we came to depend on having that coconut each year.'

Miss Douglas also comments on the Alnwick Flower Show in August, 'My twin sister was keen on cooking – she did the technical course at school – and won prizes for her girdle scones and singin' hinnies [another type of girdle scone]. Mother [the dressmaker to the herring girls] used to love the section: Something New from Something Old but she stopped entering after the year when she'd got a trench coat, unpicked it all, put on some turkey-red material and scalloped it and made it into a beautiful dress for my sister and they awarded the prize to some little clippie doormat. Oh, she was furious!'

Throughout the summer months, fairs and agricultural shows still take place in the county, not least of all the County Show at Corbridge over the Spring Bank Holiday weekend, and culminating in the Alwinton Show in October. Not only is there the judging of fine sheep and cattle, but there are sheepdog trials, best terrier and working dog competitions, hand-carved sticks ('dressed' is the local term) and shepherds' crooks; marquees packed with home-produced cakes and jams, and entertainments of all sorts.

The Duchess of Northumberland at Alnwick Flower Show, September 1934.

In October, there are also the Harvest suppers. 'Oh, we still have Harvest Home here in Beadnell. A big supper and someone with a fiddle and someone with an accordion or concertina.' (May Douglas)

31 October was also Halloween. There was no 'tricking

or treating', but the Eve of All Hallows (the evening before the Feast of All Saints on 1 November) was celebrated with lanterns made from turnips (swedes), rather than the pumpkins of today. There would be small parties where apples were floated in a tin bath and partygoers ducked their heads in the bath and tried to grab an apple with their teeth. Known as 'dookie apple', it was a young people's game, most probably because few older people had enough, if any, of their own teeth to bite into a floating apple. It was a very wet and satisfying game and remembered fondly by many of the contributors. Traditionally, trays of home-made toffee were also made at Halloween.

Guy Fawkes: 5 November: 'We had just a few fireworks and the church might have a bonfire. We'd bake potatoes in the ashes and Mother would make toffee apples. I suppose we had a guy but I don't remember that.' (Margaret Douglas)

'Some children would make a guy and wheel it round in an old pram. They'd sing. 'Christmas is coming, The goose is getting fat. Please put a penny in the old man's hat. If you haven't got a penny, a ha'penny will do. If you haven't got a ha'penny, God bless you.' (Ada Foggin)

'The Shepherds' Meet was held in November. My uncle used always to wear the Northumbrian black and white plaid to the Meet – just like the Duke's piper still wears [the Duke of Northumberland's piper plays the Northumbrian small pipes at Alnwick Castle, the Duke's Northumbrian Seat. The plaid, also known as the Shepherd's Plaid is a small black and white check]. The shepherds were all good fiddlers and they'd bring their fiddles to play for the dance. Their wives would bring food. It would go on all night until morning and the only thing that would worry them would be if it started to snow. They'd still go, carrying the children on their shoulders, but it made it harder.' (Florence Dunn)

Christmas: in those days, children's expectations, even amongst the more affluent, were much more modest. Mildred Wright of Wooler reports, 'We hung our stockings by the fireplace in the morning room. On Christmas morning they would contain an apple, an orange, a sixpence piece and perhaps some knitted blankets for a doll's cot. Although I do remember my little sister getting a big doll.'

'Oh, people made things for one another. I remember

Northumbrian pipes at the North Tyne Show, 1934.

making lavender bags with some organdie I'd bought. Sometimes I'd embroider handkerchiefs. They were always small gifts. As children we'd get dolls' clothes my mother had made, or a box of paints which never had a decent brush. There were tiny blocks of colour in the box with lovely names printed beneath them: hooker green, ultramarine, burnt umber, rose madder, imperial purple. When I became a teacher, I always encouraged the children to make small gifts at Christmas.' (Margaret Douglas).

Each year Jimmy Ditchburn's Christmas presents were, 'a new belt, a new jersey, an apple, an orange, a few nuts and a 6d.' (Jimmy's father, you recall, had died of appendicitis in 1927, when Jimmy was three years old. His mother never remarried.) 'The house would be decorated with paper streamers and I'd be sent down to the Store [the large Ashington Co-operative shop] to beg for two hoops from a butter barrel. These would be fitted at right angles one inside the other and elaborately decorated with tinsel and greenery'.

The 'Store', Seaton Hirst Co-op, near Ashington, around 1900.

Margaret Douglas also remembered being sent to the Store for hoops; a welcome errand since she loved Amble Co-operative and has vivid memories of it. 'The manager always wore a very white apron and worked at a sloping desk where he'd take the money. The men in the drapery department were very superior because they wore suits. At Christmas, the butchery department would have an elaborate display. In the centre of the window there was a suckling pig's head, with an apple in its mouth. Roland, the butcher, who always wore a striped apron and a straw hat, added a sprig of holly to his

hatband at Christmas; he would change the apple in the pig's mouth each day. He told the children it was because the pig ate it up when he wasn't looking.'

For Mrs Turnbull, there was always a Christmas party to which she could invite her schoolfriends. Apples would be hung from ceiling beams and again had to be grasped in the teeth – this version of the game was known as 'sacky apple'.

Mrs Buglass sums it up, 'We were more innocent. Small things amused us and we did not expect much.'

Goodbyes

'Six black horses with plumes.
The family got a coach, everyone else walked behind.'

Finally, dealing with death: a subject all too familiar in an age when cures were less certain and life more fleeting. National Statistics show that the mortality rate was 22.5 deaths per 1000 in the 1860s; 16 deaths per 1000 in 1901 and had declined to 11 deaths per 1000 in 2001, half of the mid-19th century level.

All the same, only the feckless failed to provide for their unexpected demise. Penny insurances were taken out as soon as it was possible. During the 19th century cases of suspected infanticide, in order to collect on insurance policies, had resulted in changes in the law so that newborns could not be insured until they reached their first birthdays. Families would struggle to maintain payment for burial clubs, however difficult this might prove to be.

Jimmy Ditchburn, although only three years old, remembers his father's Ashington funeral quite clearly, 'There were six black horses with black plumes. The man driving the hearse didn't know it was my father who'd died until he reached the front door. He was really upset because he'd been a good friend of my father's. The family mourners got a coach, but everyone else walked behind. Daylight wasn't allowed in the house until you got back from the cemetery. Even though there was insurance, families could get into a lot of debt over a funeral.'

A neighbour of Florence Wood's drove the hearse in Blyth. It was a landau – a four-wheeled, horse-drawn open carriage. Sometimes he was allowed the use of it for a day, at which time he'd take Mrs Wood's family from Blyth to Whitley Bay. She and her brother and sister loved sitting on top with the driver and she well remembers losing her new felt hat on such a trip.

'There were men who were like professional mourners, you could say. Wearing dark suits, hats and gloves, they attended all of the funerals and people would say they went for 'a lang walk and a cup of tea'. When somebody in the

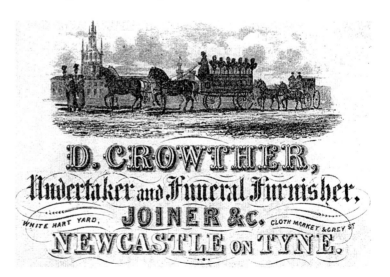

house died, first of all you'd close all the curtains, then you'd cover the mirrors with a cloth and, if you'd a fanlight over the front door, that got covered too. Mourning cards would be given out. The body of the deceased would lie in the front parlour for three days and all your friends and neighbours would come round to see the body and pay their last respects to the deceased, but also to talk to the bereaved family. It sounds ghoulish nowadays, but in fact it was kind, for it gave the bereaved a chance to talk about whoever they'd lost.

Meanwhile, the callers or bidders would have gone out to tell people where and when the funeral would be and where the wake was to be held.

On the day of the funeral, all the women, except for the widow, would stay behind to prepare the funeral tea – usually ham sandwiches and some fruit cake. Women didn't go to funerals then. The men would line up behind the hearse and they'd all walk to the church. Wherever the hearse passed, menfolk would doff their caps and bow their heads in respect for the dead. The mourners all attended the burial, I can't recall any cremations in those days. Then they'd come back to the house for the wake. Sometimes, if it was a posh funeral, the tea would be at the Co-op Hall, but most people couldn't afford that and would just have people back to the house. Whilst the men had been out, the women would have taken down the mirror coverings and opened the curtains.' (Florence Wood)

'If it was a close family member, you'd be in formal mourning for up to a year. You wore only dark clothes and you weren't allowed to go out to the cinema or even the church dances. Anything at all like that would have been considered disrespectful and would have scandalised people back then.' (Mrs Sparke)

'You'd wear black. But in some ways it was easier. Nowadays, if somebody has lost their husband or wife recently, you've no way of knowing. They'll be wearing their normal clothes, with not even a black armband to indicate their loss, and not knowing, you can put your foot in it very easily.' (Mrs Turnbull)

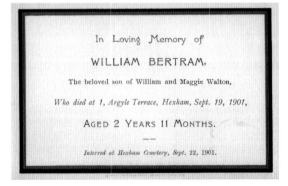

In Loving Memory of
WILLIAM BERTRAM,
The beloved son of William and Maggie Walton,
Who died at 1, Argyle Terrace, Hexham, Sept. 19, 1901,
AGED 2 YEARS 11 MONTHS.
——
Interred at Hexham Cemetery, Sept. 22, 1901.

People and places

The people in this book were born throughout the county. Some Northumberland towns may be well known, some villages and hamlets less familiar.

Alnwick: 34 miles north of Newcastle is roughly halfway between Newcastle and Berwick. Alnwick sits above the River Aln and was recently voted the best place to live in Britain. It retains much of its medieval character. At the beginning of the 20th century, Alnwick was the centre of a prosperous agricultural area, connected by the Alnwick-Coldstream branch line to the LNER London-Edinburgh main line. Hiring fairs were held twice a year. Now it has an annual, week-long fair. (Birthplace of Mrs Bolam, born 1912, a solicitor's daughter; Mrs Hindmarsh, born 1900; Isabella Keen, born 1902, a hind's daughter; Alice Sanderson, born 1900, a policeman's daughter.)

Amble: at the mouth of the River Coquet, 25 miles north of Newcastle. In 1900 it was the outlet for coals from the North Northumberland coalfields – over half a million tons were shipped out annually. Coal exports peaked in the 1920s but there was a gradual decline until the 1960s when the last pit in the area closed and the coal staithes were dismantled.

Alnwick in about 1920.

Margaret Aitken

Margaret Douglas, born in Amble, 1902.

Amble, around 1900.

There was also a brisk trade during the herring season and Amble is still an important fishing centre. (Birthplace of Margaret Douglas, born 1902, a miner's daughter).

Ashington: 16 miles north of Newcastle and three miles from the sea, Ashington once claimed to be the largest mining village in the world. At the beginning of the 19th century the area was called Felham Down but when Ashington colliery opened in 1867, the village grew up rapidly. The miners and their families lived in long, terraced 'Colliery Rows' (pronounced 'raas' by the locals, who speak a form of Geordie dialect known as 'Pitmatic' which is virtually unintelligible to strangers). The pit closed in 1988. Ashington produced more international soccer players than any other comparable place (Jim Adamson, Jack Milburn, Sir Bobby Charlton, Jack Charlton). It is also the home town of international cricketer Steve Harmison, 'The Ashington Express'. (Birthplace of Jimmy Ditchburn, born 1924, a gardener's son; Betsy Simpson, born 1907, a miner's daughter, was brought here from Stoke on Trent as a baby.)

Bamburgh: 51 miles north of Newcastle and the most popular tourist destination on the Northumbrian coast. Bamburgh castle perches on a basalt outcrop with magnificent views of the Farne Islands and Holy Island (Lindisfarne) to the east and the Cheviot Hills to the west. From AD547 Bamburgh was the capital of the ancient kingdom of Northumbria; despite the depredations of the Norsemen and the Scots, it remained independent until Norman times. (Birthplace of May Douglas, born 1920, a hind's daughter.)

Beadnell: 46 miles north of Newcastle, the village of Beadnell lies just inland and half a mile from its own harbour.

Bamburgh.

Bedlington: on the River Blyth, four miles from Ashington and 12 from Newcastle, Bedlington is famous throughout the world for its breed of dog: the Bedlington Terrier. The coming of railways brought railmaking and locomotive-building to the town. Bedlington was also a coal town and at the annual Miners' Gala numerous brass bands played and jazz bands marched. The last pit closed in 1974. (Birthplace of Mr Robinson, born 1918, a miner's son.)

Berwick upon Tweed: roughly midway between Newcastle and Edinburgh. At the mouth of the River Tweed, Berwick is a walled town which changed its nationality 13 times in 400 years, finally becoming English in 1482. Technically, having been included in the declaration of the Crimean War, but omitted from the Peace Treaty, Berwick is still at war with Russia. The Tweed is spanned by three bridges: Old Bridge, the Royal Tweed Bridge and the Royal Border Bridge. The latter is a railway bridge, built by Robert Stephenson and opened by Queen Victoria in 1850. (Mrs Buglass, born 1902, a butcher's daughter, is from Berwick upon Tweed.)

Blagdon: just off the A1, 8 miles north of Newcastle and close to Stannington. It is the estate village of Blagdon Hall, home of Viscount Ridley. (Birthplace of Evelyn Telfer, born 1914, a hind's daughter.)

Blyth: on the estuary of the River Blyth, the town was an extremely busy coal port. In the 17th century what is reputed to be the first English railway was laid down from Bebside colliery to the river; coal wagons were drawn along parallel beams of wood by horses. Ship-building and ship-repairing were also important activities. (Florence Wood, born 1914, a dock worker's daughter, is from Blyth.)

Broomhill and East Chevington: the villages of North and South Broomhill, Red Row, Hadston and Togston lie just off the A1098, three miles south of Amble and roughly 22 miles north of Newcastle. Broomhill Pit – closed in the 1970s – was once the largest pit in Northumberland. Broomhill had a railway station from which trains ran to Amble and Alnwick. The village of East Chevington, a neighbouring community, mainly of mining families, was razed to the ground after the closure of the drift mine. (Ethel Elliott was born near Red Row in the 1920s; Ned Thompson, born 1918, a miner's son, was born in East Chevington.)

Chathill: approximately 50 miles north of Newcastle and 25 miles south of Berwick. Chathill is a small settlement on the main line from London to Edinburgh. A branch line once ran to North Sunderland. (Sally H., born 1902, a railway linesman's daughter is from Chathill.)

Bedlington Market Place.

Blyth around 1910.

Choppington: a former mining settlement roughly 12 miles north of Newcastle. (Mrs Robinson, born 1920 is from Choppington.)

Coldrife: 21 miles from Newcastle and roughly five miles from Rothbury in Coquetdale. Coldrife is within sight of the southern end of the Simonside Hills, close to the switchback ups and downs on the B6342. In the early part of the 20th century the settlement was more accessible since a branch line of the Wansbeck Valley Railway ran from Morpeth to Rothbury and there was a station at Fontburn, three miles (on foot) away. (Rob McKenna, born 1902, a stonemason's son, is from Coldrife.)

Cullercoats: a tiny picturesque fishing village between Tynemouth and Whitley Bay, 9 miles east of Newcastle; once famed for its traditional fleet of 'cobles' used for inshore fishing. Cullercoats fishwives, dressed in traditional costume and carrying wicker baskets (known as creels) full of fish were well-known in the streets of nearby towns.

East Chevington: see Broomhill.

East Wilkwood: has a lonely, isolated setting in Upper Coquetdale beyond Alwinton, approximately 44 miles from Newcastle and 12 from Rothbury. It is the last village in the Coquet Valley before the land ranges off into the Cheviot Hills. East Wilkwood is now within MOD Firing Ranges and therefore inaccessible. It is described as a 'ruin' on OS maps. (Tom Dunn, born 1907, a shepherd's son is from East Wilkwood.)

Haltwhistle: 36 miles from Newcastle and 20 from Carlisle. An old market town lying one mile south of the line of Hadrian's Wall on the south-western edge of Tynedale.

Haltwhistle, around 1910.

Harbottle: roughly seven miles from Rothbury. Harbottle Castle, built 1160 became extremely important in the mid-14th century when the Lord Warden of the Middle March made it his headquarters in order to quell the rebellious, thieving natives known as 'border reivers'. On nearby Harbottle Crag is the Drake Stone (or Dragon Stone) which was once believed to cure sick children who were passed over it. Druidic rites were said to have taken place there.

Haydon Bridge: a south Tynedale village, 28 miles from Newcastle and birthplace of the artist John Martin (1789). (Janet Robinson, born 1898, is from Haydon Bridge.)

Henshaw: the hamlets of Henshaw, Redburn, Tow House and Thorngrafton are all very close to Bardon Mill village. Henshaw is an old settlement on the north bank of the River South Tyne. Tower House, which probably gives its name to the hamlet of Tow House, is a fortified farm. Until recently, a ford crossed the river here and in the 15th century a watch was kept against invading Scots who seemed to have no difficulty in surmounting Hadrian's Wall, only a couple of miles to the north. On the south bank of the river, looking rather like a small castle, is the fortified farm of Willimoteswick. (Frances Lamb, born 1900, a miner's daughter, was born in Redburn. Ruth Forster's family, farmers and blacksmiths, have lived in the area for generations.)

Frances Lamb at 100.

Hexham: 20 miles west of Newcastle has a long history. Wilfred, a monk of Lindisfarne, was given the land on which to build Hexham Abbey by Queen Ethelreda in 674 AD.

Keenley: a tiny hamlet in West Allendale and 20 miles by road from Hexham; former lead-mining country. (Mrs Sparke, born 1914, a miner's daughter, is from Keenley.)

Kidlandlee: high in Coquetdale, on the south side of the Cheviot Hills. (Florence Dunn, born 1909, a shepherd's daughter is from Kidlandlee.)

Lesbury: a village, five miles from Alnwick, on the road to Alnmouth.

Linn Briggs: two-and-a-half miles upstream from Alwinton, in Upper Coquetdale, where there are two bridges over the the River Coquet. The surrounding hills with their traces of ancient settlements have wonderfully evocative names: Witch Crags, Slippery Crags, Quickening Cote, Copper Snout and Lord's Seat. (Tom Dunn, born 1907 at East Wilkwood, mentions Linn Briggs in a story he tells.)

Longframlington: between Morpeth and Alnwick.

Longhoughton: about four miles east of Alnwick; the main line railway to Edinburgh once stopped at this small agricultural and quarrying village. (Home of Mrs Cassie, born 1904.)

Melkridge: a small, picturesque hamlet close to Haltwhistle. (Mrs Turnbull, born 1916, a master sinker's daughter is from Melkridge.)

Morpeth: now the county town, nestles in a loop of the Wansbeck, about 15 miles north of Newcastle.

Netherwitton: in a sheltered valley eight miles or so west of Morpeth. (Betty Robson, born 1903, a coachman's daughter, is from Netherwitton.)

Newbiggin: 16 miles north-east of Newcastle. An ancient village dating from the 12th century and an extremely important little port in medieval times. It declined into a small fishing village where boats were (and still are) drawn straight up onto the beach. The coming of the railway in the 19th century made it easily accessible from Tyneside and it became popular as a holiday venue. In the later part of the 20th cen-

Newbiggin, around 1910. The coast is now much eroded.

tury the line closed and due to erosion the coastline began to collapse into the sea. (Home of Lizzie Voersing, born 1908, a fisherman's daughter; Maggie Brown, born 1898, a fisherman's daughter; Mrs Cox, born 1905, a shopkeeper's daughter; Christopher Blandford, born 1920, a miner's son.)

Newton by the Sea: 46 miles north of Newcastle. (Home of Mr Price, born 1900, a farmer's son.)

North Shields: six miles east of Newcastle and now part of North Tyneside. By mid-19th century, North Shields was an extremely busy port with a large fishing fleet and smokehouses for the kippering of herring. The late 20th century saw a decline in the fishing industry and its allied trades. (Home of Bob Duff, born 1910, son of a trawlerman; Margaret Compson, born 1918.)

North Sunderland: 48 miles north of Newcastle. An ancient coastal settlement. A branch railway line ran from Chathill from 1898 until 1951. (Home of May Telfer, born 1903, a farmworker's daughter.)

W. Telfer

May Telfer.

Pegswood: a colliery village two miles east of Morpeth, on the road to Ashington. (Home of Barbara Coulthard, born 1904, a miner's daughter.)

Redburn: see Henshaw.

Red Row: see Broomhill.

Seahouses: 48 miles north of Newcastle and gateway to the Farne Islands. The harbour was enlarged in the mid-19th century to serve the herring fishing.

Seaton Delaval: eight miles north-east of Newcastle, and a mile from the coast. The former home of the Delaval family. The hall, designed by Vanburgh, was built in 1728. (Home of Ada Foggin, born 1908, whose father abandoned the family and emigrated to Australia.)

Seaton Sluice: developed as a harbour by the Delavals to export coal from their mines. A busy industrial community, which included a glassworks, its coal trade was overtaken by newer and bigger harbours at Blyth and on the Tyne.

Tynemouth: seaside town, eight miles east of Newcastle. (Home of Minnie Craighead, born 1912, a superintendent engineer's daughter.)

Whitley Bay: 10 miles north east of Newcastle and once Tyneside's most popular seaside resort. (Mentioned by Florence Wood, born 1914, from Blyth.)

Whittonstall: on the border between County Durham and Northumberland. A small hilltop hamlet, four-and-a-half miles south of Stocksfield on the Roman road known as Dere Street. (Home of Elizabeth Ann Luck, born 1912, daughter of a hind.)

Wooler: 48 miles north west of Newcastle. From 1887 to 1930 the Alnwick to Coldstream branch line of the LNER served the thinly-populated but large area east of the Cheviot Hills. An important market town, with a fine main street, Wooler was noted for its sheep sales. (Home of Mildred Wright, born in 1912, a bank manager's daughter and Olive Purves, born in 1905, daughter of a tobacconist and keen photographer.)

Barbara Wright

Mildred Wright.

Some Northumbrian dialect words

Arles – payment as contract of a hiring
Baist – to beat or thrash
Bairn – a child
Bait – a packed lunch
Bank – a steep incline
Beck – a small stream
Bigg – barley (as in the Bigg Market, Newcastle)
Blabb – to reveal a secret
Blather – talk nonsense
Bonny – beautiful (also implies healthy)
Bubble – to weep
Cadge – to borrow
Canny – generous, good, gentle, kind
Chare – a narrow lane
Chiggies – small coals for a fire
Claggy – sticky (as in toffee)
Clarts – slippery mud
Clip – to smack
Clippie mat – a small rug made from strips of old clothing.
Clout – a hard blow, but also a cloth as in dish clout.
Coup – turn upside down (rhymes with clout)
Couping yer creel – turning a somersault
Cracket – a small stool
Dad – a blow, or as a verb, to deliver a blow.
Dook – to duck one's head
Fret – mist, particularly sea mist
Funning – teasing, or enjoying a joke
Gannin' – going
Gansey – a fisherman's sweater
Geet – great (as in 'geet big' or very large)
Gerrit – frame around the waist from which to hang buckets
Girdle – ditto, but also a flat, circular iron plate, with handles, on which to cook scones over the open fire.

Haem – home (pronounced 'yem')
Hadaway – equivalent of 'You don't say'
Heed – the head
Hind – farm labourer, usually annually contracted
Hinny – a term of endearment
Hooky mat – similar to a clippie mat
Hoyin' – throwing
Howkin' – digging
Jarp – to strike
Keppin' – catching
Laidley – horrible, loathsome (as in the Laidley Worm)
Lardy cake – bread dough enriched with butter and dried fruit
Lonnen – a lane
Loupin' – jumping
Marrer – a workmate (especially in the pits)
Mizzle – fine rain, wet mist
Nark – to annoy
Neb(n) – a small, steel stud for work boots. Verb to be very nosy
Netty – the lavatory
Pant – a public water fountain
Plodge – to wade ankle-deep
Set Pot – a large, fixed copper pot with space for a fire beneath it
Skairn – to open a mussel
Spuggy – a sparrow, but can also mean any bird
Stot – to bounce
Stotty – a flat loaf baked on the floor of the oven
Stooks – corn sheaves
Teem – to pour down
Tappy-lappy – to rush off
Yetlin – a cast iron cooking pot hung from a hook above a fire

Index to the contributors